WILMA ELLERSIEK

GNOMES AND GIANTS, PIXIES AND ELVES
Hand Gesture and Movement Games for Young Children

TRANSLATED AND EDITED BY
KUNDRY WILLWERTH, LYNN ST. PIERRE, AND SOMER SERPE

WITH CONTRIBUTIONS BY
BIRGIT KROHMER AND INGRID WEIDENFELD

WALDORF EARLY CHILDHOOD ASSOCIATION OF NORTH AMERICA

Acknowledgments

This publication was made possible by a grant from the Waldorf Curriculum Fund.

Selection, preparation and translation of the original German texts, songs, and games were made possible in part by a grant from the International Waldorf Kindergarten Association.

Translated from the German edition, *Zwerge, elfen und andere kleine Wesen* by Wilma Ellersiek, Verlag Freies Geistesleben, Stuttgart. Copyright © 2017 Verlag Freies Geistesleben & Urachhaus, GmbH, Stuttgart, Germany.

This English translation copyright © Waldorf Early Childhood Association of North America, 2023.

Published by
Waldorf Early Childhood Association of North America (WECAN)
285 Hungry Hollow Road, Spring Valley, New York 10977 USA.

ISBN: 978-1-936849-60-4

Illustrations: Friedericke Lötgers and Magdalena Gadaj
Musical notations: Ingrid Weidenfeld
Design and typeset: Lory Widmer Hess
(based on the series design by Roland Willwerth)

All rights reserved. No part of this book may be reproduced in any form without the written permission of the publisher, except for brief quotations in book reviews and articles.

Printed in the United States of America

Table of Contents

Introduction
Foreword by Birgit Krohmer ... vii
Foreword by Wilma Ellersiek ... ix
Musicalized Speech by Ingrid Weidenfeld ... xi
Notes on playing the Choroi Flute ... xii
General Notes on Musical Notation ... xiii

The Games
The Root Gnome (Basic Game) ... 14
The Root Gnome: Expansion Game I ... 16
In the meadows and in the garden
The Root Gnome: Expansion Game II ... 20

Elves Game I
Elves Care for the Little Flower ... 22
Elves Game II
Elves Dance in the Moonlight ... 26

Sleepy: Mood of the Fifth song ... 30

To Be an Elf Child ... 32

In the Mountain ... 33

In Woodland a Soft Crack! ... 40
The Wind Blows Through the Trees ... 46

The Pixie Dance ... 48
The Pixie Dance (Under the Spiderweb Tent) ... 53

Scoot ... 54
Scoot's Dream Song ... 60
What Scoot Does in Wintertime ... 64

Who Tromps Around Through All the Wood? ... 68
Rommelgood's Tromping Song ... 71
Quiet Diddledoo ... 74

Song of Trolls and Gnomes ... 75
Noll the Troll ... 76
Noll the Troll Is Resting! ... 80

The Waterman ... 83
Mermaid in the Moonlight ... 88
The Mermaid's Dream ... 96

The Playful Hobgoblin ... 99
The Hobgoblin Dance ... 103

Will o' the Wisps ... 109

The Little Ghosts o' Night ... 111
The Little Ghosts o' Night II ... 117

Appendices
Recommendations for Companion/Bridge Verses ... 121
Wilma Ellersiek, a Life for Rhythm ... 123
Contributors ... 125
Addresses ... 126

FOREWORD

by Birgit Krohmer

Translated by Susan Howard

We can often experience with children that they see and speak with elemental beings. This can be dismissed as anthropomorphism, but it can also be noticed that children sometimes like to be in certain special places and have little conversations there with "someone." Sensitive adults, too, may be able to perceive special places in nature. And we can be astonished again and again when we are desperately looking for something that is obviously exactly in a certain place somewhere, that as soon as we regain our inner equilibrium, the lost object "coincidentally" falls into our hands. We are also familiar with tales of the elves and the shoemaker, the leprechaun with his pot of gold, the tooth fairy, the "jolly old elf" Santa Claus, and Snow White and the seven dwarves, to name but a few. It is exciting to notice how many earth beings and house beings there are in different countries. In Scandinavia, for example, there are many elemental beings, from the tomten, the good spirits of houses and farms in Sweden, to the fearsome trolls in Norway. The wind beings live more in the Slavic regions, the water beings in the rice-growing cultures. Every landscape has its own special character and as a result a special way of inhabiting the elemental world. Legends, fairy tales, and poems in every part of the world tell of the original inhabitants and their encounters with human beings.

In his lectures Rudolf Steiner often spoke about elemental beings and assigned them to their elements and spheres of life. Today speaking about them has become "socially acceptable" again.

Wilma Ellersiek's games are the result of a rich life of observing and perceiving nature at a time when nature was healthier and closer to its origins. We can study the phenomena of nature again and again, in order to then integrate them into the movements of our own games. When we playfully grasp the elements, the realms of nature appear through our life forces. This is much closer to their innermost being than images or characters of any kind, in which someone has made up a picture for himself and taken it out of a living process.

Especially in today's world, where so much is brought into picture images and characters, it is a gift to learn the games from Wilma Ellersiek. Just like elemental beings, they do not have a fixed form, but live between appearing and fading, through the hand of the shaping adult. These beings thus really come to life and are never merely external images. It is precisely because children see these beings that we should beware of inventing images.

The path from the perception of the classical elements—earth, water, air and fire—to the perception of the beings who permeate these elements with life, to the feeling of the essential members of one's own being, is a modern path of initiation. This ascent from the realms of nature to nature's own living beings and then to the essential members of the human being is also shown in the corresponding words: element – elemental being – essential member (in German: *Element – Elementarwesen – Wesensglied*).

Nature is less and less approachable to us today, because of the way we humans deal with it; the pull of the media also has its effect on us. In the past, we often had to call the children inside when they were playing outdoors in the evenings; today we have to demand that they go outside. And the same usually applies to our own lifestyle. But the benefits of a walk or the enjoyment of a puddle or a ray of sunshine are still available to all of us every day.

If we take this path of learning to perceive elemental beings, we can come closer—with full consciousness—to the children, for whom this world is still open. At the same time, nature, which is increasingly cramped, threatened, and dying, can be revived by human beings.

The games of Wilma Ellersiek are a gift from the hand of the adult, who never comes empty-handed, and are thus a remedy against the anti-spirit of our times, which overwhelms children with commercial "playthings." We can always share our time with children and fill it with the whole world of elemental beings. In this way we are role models, not only for a particular game, but also—more importantly—for consciously and deliberately connecting ourselves with living nature. We have everything with us at any time and in any place!

I wish you much joy with the book and hope that exploring the elemental world and the favorite games of your children will open up new worlds for you.

"Life has nothing to do with methods. We learn from the seagulls or from small children or from growing plants what life means. We have the ability within us, as we become more and more awake, to feel more and more clearly what our own nature has to tell us." (Charlotte Selver, *Re-claiming Vitality and Presence Sensory Awareness as a Practice for Life*, North Atlantic Books 2007.)

FOREWORD
by Wilma Ellersiek

Translated by Susan Howard

How stories and games about elemental beings should be created for children in the first seven years

We must get rid of the superstition that only that which can be measured is reality. This belief leads to mental crippling.
— Medart Boss, psychoanalyst

For children in the first seven years, stories and games about elemental beings require an artistic approach to the quality of "elemental beingness." In rhythmic-musical sequences of movements (hand gestures or body gestures), combined with corresponding poetic language (verses), melodic motifs, and songs in the mood of the fifth, the child in the first seven years must be given the possibility to "slip into" the archetypal gestures of the particular elemental being. This enables the child to grasp the essence of the figures from the elemental world and to integrate them.

In their "bodily imagination" the child becomes a dwarf, gnome, giant, troll, elf, mermaid, hobgoblin, and so on, and acquires "bodily knowledge" of the particular "being like this" of each elemental being.

This embodiment of elemental beings is a form of offering appropriate linguistic and bodily gestures that must precede later soul experience and conceptual understanding. This later soul experience is conveyed through verbal images, and conceptual understanding through verbal concepts. This earlier "embodiment" is a form of learning that corresponds to the child's nature and makes possible a bodily comprehension of the world without appealing to conceptual understanding.

Why dwarves and gnomes love children

Gnomes, dwarves, elves, and hobgoblins love the tender, lovely faces of the children, because they themselves have wrinkled skin and thick noses. They are also amazed by the well-proportioned arms, hands, legs, and feet of the children—they themselves have only tiny, spindly limbs and torsos in relation to their thick heads with shaggy hair and beards. Because they can only giggle and have chirpy voices, they enjoy the bright laughter and the melodious singing of the children.

The elementals' overly clever heads and withered souls enjoy the light-hearted, imaginative play of the children. They love being close to the childlike physical body's organization, interwoven with etheric formative forces. Through this they gain vitality and joy.

There is a remarkable statement by the Dutch scientist and Waldorf teacher Frits Julius (1902-1970), who had a special relationship to the elemental beings. He mentioned that the elementals love the little children! When people speak to them about children—for example, in the forest to the gnomes and dwarves—it makes them very happy.* They show their gratitude to the person who has given them this joy by, for example, leading them to a particularly beautiful place in the forest, where one can find many ripe berries; they also let them find wonderfully fine flowers or rare stones, tasty mushrooms and soft moss and so on.

*See *From Loneliness to Connection* by Adam Bittleston, Floris Books, 2013.

Musicalized Speech

On the use of language in the rhythmic-musical speech and movement games of Wilma Ellersiek

by Ingrid Weidenfeld

Every game presented here is designed in such a way that speech has a special place in the game. It has only a secondary function of conveying content and information; first and foremost it is the carrier of the music. This creates the necessity to shape language. If one summarizes what actually constitutes music, one comes up with a few important terms: melos, rhythm and dynamics (or harmony*). All three (or four) include "agogics," a rather little-known term which describes the inner breath within each musical experience. Through agogics, single musical or spoken passages or even single notes or words can be stretched or compressed as they are being played or spoken.

The word "melody" is immediately recognizable in the term "melos" and is often associated with singing. But there is also the speech melody, which we become aware of especially when reciting poems and texts. The rhythm is characterized by the polarities of length and shortness. Already in Ancient Greece people worked very consciously with the juxtaposition of long and short syllables in different sequences. The well-known speech rhythms originate from this time: iambus, dactylus, trochee, anapest.

* Harmony in the true sense is reserved for music; in language it is hidden in rhyme.

Dynamics shape the music by means of volume and emphasis. If every piece of music were to be played at the same volume from beginning to end, the listener would soon no longer feel like listening to this boring sound.

So, too, in language. In everyday life we deal with these design elements quite unconsciously. Once we consciously pay attention to them, we soon notice that we have a great deal of leeway in volume and emphasis. Wilma Ellersiek's concern is to enable children to experience rhythmic and musical sound through language. Nevertheless, language comes in second place: it "only" accompanies the movements. Children's learning is body-centered, that is, everything children feel and grasp in the sense of touching, what they touch and experience with their body through their own movement, forms knowledge.

Rhythmic-musical speech and movement games are designed in such a way that an adult, be it the mother, father, grandmother or grandfather, or educator, shows a game thoroughly prepared, so that the child can enter into the process of movement through imitation and at the same time experience the musical language as a unified act of speaking and moving. In this sense, Wilma Ellersiek originally wrote a sentence above every game:

Speech must be designed in such a way that language can be experienced as movement and sound activity, highlighting sound and rhythm.

Or:

It is important to design language in such a way that it is a rhythmic-musical activity and can be experienced as movement and sound. Very musical, that means not speaking in the ordinary everyday language, but using language rhythmically, often calling or almost singing.

Or:

When speaking, emphasize rhythm and melos (melody), so that the language is experienced as movement and sound and can stimulate movement.

It takes practice to implement all these suggestions. Despite these indications, the language should convey lightness. It should not be dramatic, and the emotions of the speaker should not be allowed to resonate. Childlike cheerfulness is the basic mood that can be conveyed through language in every game.

Notes on movement and gestures

Just as Wilma Ellersiek has given various suggestions for the use of language in her games, she has also given information about the movements. She herself was always in search of the archetypal gesture, that is, the gesture that comes closest to the phenomenon. With untiring enthusiasm Ellersiek observed the flowers, the animals, the course of the year with its manifold natural phenomena, and listened to the wind, the water, the rain. Out of all this observation she tried to find the true gesture. It wasn't enough for her to show something that "roughly" corresponded. From her observations she developed a great wealth of finely differentiated movement sequences. This phrase already contains the secret: it is a process, a constantly changing, developing process. The player does not show states in still gestures, but lets the movements come into being and pass away again. It is not about the finished gesture, but about the process of creation. That is why a similarly formulated sentence was to be found again and again for the movement sequences above each game:

The gestures must always be prepared well, i.e. before speaking, so that movement and speaking can happen together. You have to take your time for the slow movements and the pauses in which, for example, you look at the 'blossom' or change from one movement to another.

Or:

Prepare movements well, so that speech and movement are experienced as one act.

NOTES ON PLAYING THE CHOROI FLUTE

Let the tone sound completely on the flowing breath, without activating the tip of the tongue (not like the "doot-doot" on the recorder). To produce the tone, breathe into the flute and let the tone glide along the stream of the breath so that the child can perceive it as a caress (i.e., no activity of the tip of the tongue). Swing according to the melodic vibration.

GENERAL NOTES ON MUSICAL NOTATION

The music is not meant to conform to any standard meter or measurable notation value. Rather, it is intended as a reminder of the melody line. One sings freely, following the flow of speech and movement, without being tied to the length or shortness of the notes or to bar arrangements. The speech process determines the rhythmic and dynamic progression.

● ≈ 1 basic beat, a pulsation based on the heartbeat in the streaming, swinging musical action, without a division into bars by accentuation or any established meter. Sing following the language, maintaining a calm rhythmic swinging, which can slow down at the end of a song.

THE ROOT GNOME (BASIC GAME)
Rhythmic-musical hand gesture game

Zoop - zoop!
The root gnome cleans with skill
the little roots within the hill.
Zoop-zoop, zoop-zoop. Zoop-zoop!
And from the earthly bower
grows forth a little flower.
It opens in the sunshine -
    ————————————— (silent movement)
Ohhhhh!
So fragrant, ah, wo---nderfine!
    ————————————— (silent movement)
Ah- ah-
ahhh - choo! -
Choo!
Thank you, flower mine!

Text
Speech must be formed so that gestures and sound are experienced rhythmically and musically.

1. Zoop- zoop!
    T   **T**
  The root gnome cleans with skill
    P   **P**   M   **M**   **R**
  the lit-tle roots with-in the hill.
   PI **PI** T T   P   **P**   M **M**
  Zoop-zoop, zoop-zoop. Zoop-zoop!
    R   **R**   PI **PI** T   **T**

2. And from the earthly bower

Gestures
Prepare gestures well before speaking, so that speech always coincides with the gesture.

1. The right hand hangs down loosely just above the right thigh. Starting with the right thumb, the left fingertips and thumb encircle the base of the right thumb and draw out past the fingertip, as if removing a little gnome hat. The second time is more emphasized, with the movement drawing just over the fingertips, and more prominent in speech. Repeat this gesture with the right pointer, middle finger, ring finger, and pinkie - then pass behind the fingers back to the thumb and repeat this sequence again, then pass behind the fingers to end with the thumb! The rhythm of accenting the second syllable is continued throughout this entire section of verse.

2. Slowly turn the right hand while making a soft fist, with the thumb lying on the fingers, until the back of the hand lies on the middle thigh. At the same time, speak the accompanying text slowly and in an elongated way, particularly the "ow" in "bower." Movement and speech must end together.

3. groooooows fooooorth

4. a little flower.

5. It opens in the sunshine -

6. (Silent)
      x

7. Ohhhhh! (voiceless exhale)

8. So fragrant, ah, wo---nderfine!
      v   *v*

9. (Silent)
      x

10. Ah- ah-
       ahhh - choo!
       Choooo!

11. Thank you, flower mine!
               v

---

3. With fingernails slide along the inside of the thumb until all the ends of the fingers touch the end of the thumb—the fingers and thumb are all vertical, reaching toward the sun. Movements are smooth, along with the elongated sounds of the vowels.

4. Right hand, as bud, moves upward (the flower grows), still with fingertips up until chest height. Slowly, say "flower" in an elongated way, almost singing. Silently watch bud.

5. Open fingers and hand very slowly. Speak melodiously, keeping voice high. Silently watch the blossom.

6. Bend down to gently smell the blossom. Lift head to look at the children, enchanted by the fragrance.

7. Exhale a voiceless "Ohhhhh!"

8. Gaze back at the blossom and say, "So fragrant, ah, wonderfine!" extending the vowel "o". Nod head slightly at each *v*.

9. Smell the blossom once more, gently, slowly. Lift head to look at the children, and as before enchanted by the fragrance, get ready to exhale "Ohhhhh!

10. Instead take a sudden, short in breath changing into "Ah - ah -". Then a long in breath "Ahhh" and exhale air with "Choo!" and the longer "Choooo!" The sequence of sneezing is rhythmical-musical.

"Ah - ah"	Rhythm: short - short Tone: same tone
"Ahhh - Choo!"	Rhythm: long - short Tone: low - high
"Choooo!"	Rhythm: long Tone: very high

11. Smile at the children, perhaps a little laugh. Look at the blossom and gently "cover" it with your soft open hand. Nod gently at *v*.

x smell flower, breathe in the fragrance carefully
v nod

After it has been played more often, the basic game, "The Root Gnome," can be expanded, first by adding parts A and C and/or parts B and C. This expanded version I is an artistically designed form of indirect repetition. Finally, to further enrich the game, one can add the expanded version II with parts D and E. In this way, the children who would like the repetition will be satisfied and those who do not want the repetition will be taken into the repetition without realizing it.

The hand gesture game, "The Root Gnome," can also be expanded into a circle game, whether the basic game is played alone or with the expanded versions that the children know.

THE ROOT GNOME: EXPANSION GAME I
In the meadows and in the garden

A

Not only in the hill
the root gnomes pull with skill;
in the meadow they pull as well.
Let me tell:
they're cleaning every little root.
Zoop-zoop, zoop-zoop,
so soft and good.
Zoop-zoop, zoop-zoop, zoop-zoop!
And from the earthly bower
grows forth a little flower...etc.

B

Not only in the meadow,
not only in the hill,
the root gnomes pull with skill.
In the garden they pull now.
And already, you know how:
they're cleaning every little root.
Zoop-zoop, zoop-zoop,
so soft and good.
Zoop-zoop, zoop-zoop, zoop-zoop!
And from the earthly bower
grows forth a little flower...etc.

C (ending)

And thank you to the gnomes
in the garden, meadow, and hill,
who pull the roots with skill.
Thank you! Thank you! Thank you!

A: Text

1a. Not only in the hill

1a

2a. the root gnomes

3a. pull with skill;
    ////   ////

4a. in the meadow they pull as well. Let me tell:

5a. they're clean-ing ev-ery lit-tle root.
    T   **T**   P **P** **M** M R **R**
Zoop-zoop, zoop-zoop,
    PI **PI**   T   **T**
so soft and good.
    P **P** M **M**
Zoop-zoop, zoop-zoop, zoop-zoop!
    R   **R**   PI **PI** T   **T**

And from the earthly bower
Grows forth a little flower...

A: Gestures

1a. Raise hands overhead with fingertips touching, indicating a hill.

2a

2a. Indicate a pointed cap with thumbs resting on head and fingertips touching each other.

3a. The right hand hangs loosely over right thigh, fingers pointed downward.
    Here, pull the fingers of the right hand with fingers of the left hand, twice at "pull" and "skill."

4a. On the word "meadow," indicate with palms facing the floor, a flat meadow in front of knees.

5a. For hand gestures for the rest of the game, refer to the basic game starting with 1. After completion, you can continue with the expansion game.

B: Text

1b. Not only in the meadow,

2b. not only in the hill,
    the root gnomes pull with skill.

3b. In the garden they pull now,
    And already, you know how:

4b. they're clean-ing ev-ery lit-tle root.
    T   **T**   P **P** M **M** R **R**
Zoop-zoop, zoop-zoop,
    PI **PI** T   **T**
So soft and good.
    P **P** M **M**
Zoop-zoop, zoop-zoop, zoop-zoop!
    R **R** PI **PI** T **T**

5b. And from the earthly bower
    grows forth a little flower…etc.

B: Gestures

1b. At the word "meadow," indicate with palms facing the floor, a flat meadow in front of knees.

2b. At the word "hill," lift hands over head with fingertips touching, indicating a hill. At the word "gnomes," indicate a pointed cap with thumbs resting on head and fingertips touching each other (see pictures above). Here, pull the fingers of the right hand twice with fingers of the left hand, at "pull" and "skill."

3b. Show a garden with both hands—palms facing the children—moving left and right arms away from each other around knees towards the back.

4b. Now pull fingers of right hand again with fingers of left hand (as in basic game at 1).

5b. For hand gestures, refer to the basic game, "The Root Gnome," which is played through from here to end. After completion, you can continue with the complementary game C.

C: Text

1c. And thank you to the gnomes
          v

2c. in the garden, meadow, and hill,

3c. who pull the roots with skill.

4c. Thank you! - Thank you! - Thank you!
       left   *right*   *center*

C: Gestures

1c. At "thank you," nod head, and at "gnomes," again indicate a pointed cap with thumbs touching on top of head and fingers pointed together.

2c. Gestures are as above: for the "garden" see 3b, for the "meadow" see 1b, and for the "hill" see 2b.

3c. With the right hand, pull all fingers of the left hand at the same time twice. At "roots," let both hands hang down like roots, palms heavy, facing your body.

4c. With outstretched arms with palms up and below waist height, bow three times, letting hands relax down as you bow, to the left, right, and then center.

Note: The "thank you" to the gnomes can also find a place in Part A, but then only twice for the meadow and hill.

THE ROOT GNOME: EXPANSION GAME II

D

*Yes, in the garden, in the meadow, and in the hill
the root gnomes pull with skill.
Zoop-zoop, zoop-zoop, zoop-zoop!
And from the earthly bower
grow forth the little flowers.
They open in the sunshine.
Ohhh!- ohhh!
So fragrant, ah, wo--nderfine!
(Silent gesture.......)
Ah-ah-ahhh-choo!-Choo!
Ah-ah-ahhh-choo!-Choo!
Thank you! Thank you!
Flowers mine!*

E (ending)

*And thank you to the gnomes
in the garden, meadow, and hill
who pull the roots with skill.
Thank you! -Thank you! - Thank you!*

D: Text

1d. Yes, in the garden, in the meadow, and in the hill

2d. the root gnomes pull with skill.

Zoop-zoop, zoop-zoop, zoop-zoop!

3d. And from the earthly bower
Grow forth the little flowers.
They open in the sunshine.

4d. Ohhh!- ohhh!

5d. So fragrant, ah, wo--nderfine!

6d. [Silent gesture]

D: Gestures

1d. Follow gestures as above; for the "garden," refer to 3b. For the "meadow," refer to 1b, and for the "hill" refer to 2b.

2d. At "root gnomes," indicate a pointed cap with thumbs touching on top of head and fingers pointed together. Then, pull all fingers of the right hand with all the fingers of the left hand as marked.

3d. All gestures should follow the basic game "The Root Gnome," only this time with both hands at the same time (refer to 2-5).

4d. For the first "ohhh" smell the right hand, for the second smell the left hand.

5d. Turn to the children and speak.

6d. Again, smell the right "flower" and from here continue as described in 6 of the basic game.

7d. Ah-ah-ahhh-choo!-Choo!

8d. Ah-ah-ahhh-choo!-Choo!

9d. Thank you! Thank you!
     1   2

10d. Flowers mine!

7d. Turn to the right "flower" and continue (refer to basic game at 7).

8d. Turn to the left "flower" and continue.

9d. 1. Gently cover the right flower with the left hand
     2. Gently cover the left flower with the right hand

10d. Look at both flowers lovingly.

E: Text

1e. And thank you to the gnomes
                        v

2e. in the garden, meadow, and hill

3e. who pull the roots with skill.

4e. Thank you! - Thank you! - Thank you!
     left   *right*   *center*

E: Gestures

1e. At "thank you," nod head, and at "gnomes" again indicate a pointed cap with thumbs touching on top of head and fingers pointed together.

2e. Follow gestures as above; for the "garden," refer to 3b. For the "meadow," refer to 1b, and for the "hill" refer to 2b.

3e. With the left hand, pull all fingers of the right hand at the same time twice. At "roots," let both hands hang down like roots, palms heavy, facing your body.

4e. With arms outstretched and palms up, bow three times left, right and then center, then bring hands down.

ELVES GAME I: ELVES CARE FOR THE LITTLE FLOWER
Rhythmic-musical hand gesture game

In sunshine clear, in sunshine clear,
elf speaks to the flower dear:
"Come out of the earth below,
sprout-sprout and upward grow!
Open wide toward the sun's light,
bloom, bloom, my flower bright."

Elf speaks, "Down falls the rain.
Drink of heaven's gift again.
Troppa-droppa-droppa-droppa,
troppa-droppa-droppa-droppa."

Elf speaks to the wind so mild:
"Sway, sway, my flower child.
Soo-soo-soooo – soo-soo-soooo,
soo-soo-sooooooo!"

Elf speaks: "Now comes the night.
Flower, close your blossom tight.
Sleep-sleep and rest so still.
Flower, rest now, too.
Soo-soo-soooo, soo-soo-soooo,
sooo-soooo-sooooooo!"

Text
1. In sunshine clear, in sunshine clear,

2. Elf speaks

3. to the flower dear:

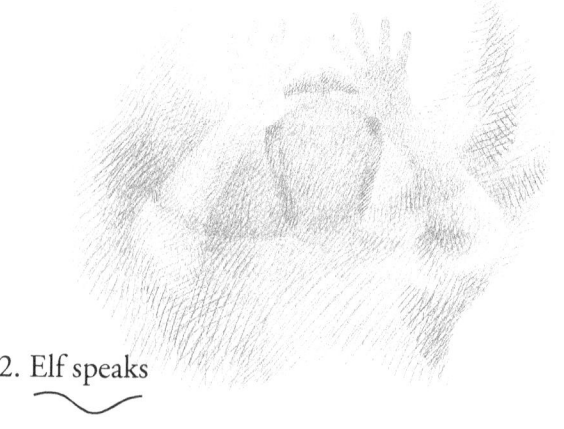

Gestures
1. Sit with the children on stools, chairs, or on knees on the floor. Starting with relaxed hands on knees, fingers curled under, backs of hands are up. Hands slowly rise like the sun with fingers slowly unfolding by chest height, arms are rounded as if holding a large ball. The hands continue rising with fingers outstretched and thumbs touching as sun rays. By the second "in sunshine clear," let the sun shine in the sky moving slightly forward and down.

2. Now spread arms like wings, not extending them all the way. Move arms loosely and lightly in the direction of the movement line shown under the text at left, up and down.

3. With both hands, form a blossom, wrists touching, fingers slightly rounded with hands held vertically upward, show an opening flower bud.

4. [Silent movement]

5. "Come out of the earth below,

6. [Silent movement]

7. sprout-sprout

8. and upward grow!

9. Open wide toward the sun's light,

10. bloom, bloom, my flower bright."

11. Elf speaks,

12. "Down falls the rain.

13. Drink of heaven's gift again.

4. Afterward, no matter if sitting in a chair or on the ground, let the gesture slowly dissolve with hands ending on the floor or thighs.

5. Now, move both hands as if wanting to pull or lift something out from the ground. Do this gesture twice, following movement arrows under the text at left.

6. With both hands, form a "bulb," wrapping right hand over left fist, and place it on the floor or your lap.

7. Very slowly, unroll fingers of the left hand, with left fingernails moving up along the fingers of the right hand, straightening them as the two hands come together in a teardrop shape with palms facing, wrists together and fingertips together pointing upward at chest height.

8. Raise the "sprout tip" higher until the wrists are at chest height.

9. There, open the fingers very slowly until it creates a blossom.

10. Hold the blossom and look at it lovingly.

11. Movement as above in 2

12. Move hands up until they are head high, the palms facing down, with fingers relaxed down below the palms of the hands. The fingers move continuously like raindrops. Move the hands with the "rain" down until the fingers reach the floor or your lap. Speak the word "rain" stretched out as that happens.

13. Form the blossom with hands (see 3 above), and hold it out to the rain.

14. [Silent movement]

15. Troppa-droppa-droppa-droppa,

16. [Silent movement]

17. Troppa-droppa-droppa-droppa."

18. [Silent movement]

19. Elf speaks

20. to the wind so mild:

21. "Swaaay, Swaaay,

22. my flower child.

23. Soo-soo-soooo - soo-soo-soooo

   Soo-soo - sooooooo!"

24. Elf speaks:

25. "Now comes the night.

26. Flower, close your blossom tight.

---

14. Raise hands above your head again

15. And let it rain like it is written above in 12.

16. Without speaking, drum fingertips as "rain" on the ground or on your thighs. On your thighs you can "feel" the rain, and on the floor you can "hear" the rain.

17. Again let it run down from above as in 12 above.

18. Repeat movement as in 16

19. Movement as above in 2

20. With palms facing each other some inches apart, and fingers directed towards children, make a light, airy wave from right to left.

21. With the same gesture show the waving from left to right, then from right to left. Stretch out the word "sway," almost singing it.

22. Show the blossom as in 3

23. Sway the blossom cup softly and tenderly (almost imperceptibly) back and forth.

24. Movement as above in 2

25. Drop your head and hold your arms with wrists crossed in an arch by your forehead, letting hands hang loosely. The gesture shows the darkness coming. Give it time.

26. Show the blossom again as in 3, then lay fingers of the right hand lightly over the fingers of the left hand that are loosely curling inward. The blossom closes itself.

27. Sleep - sleep and rest so still.

28. Flower, rest now, too.

29. Soo-soo-soooo, soo-soo-soooo,

soo-soo-sooooooo!"

27. Hold the blossom quietly and look lovingly at it while speaking.

28. Bow head forward and you can also lay your forehead on the closed blossom.*

29. Rock the blossom gently and tenderly back and forth. When the forehead touches the blossom, it too can rock back and forth with the blossom, then stay still for a little while and quietly dissolve the gesture.

* NOTE: If you would like to close with the movement game, "Elf Dancing in the Moonlight," the following text is inserted here to get ready for the game.

29. The little elf rests now too.

29. Lay hands in lap and bow head, lowering eyelids. Stay awhile like this.

30. Soo-soo-sooo - soo-soo-sooo,

sooo-soooo-sooooo.

30. Rock upper body gently, almost imperceptibly back and forth. Then stay a little while in a resting gesture. Now the elf can dance in the moonlight.

ELVES GAME II: ELVES DANCE IN THE MOONLIGHT
Rhythmic-musical movement game
(Also good as an expansion game for Elves Game I)

From blossom cup they slip away -
the elves join in a roundalay.
They fly and hover,
they wave and weave.

Flying-flying-flying-flying,
swaying-swaying,
waving-waving-waving-waving,
weaving-weaving.

"Simmmm!" There sounds a light ringing.
"Simmmm!" The flower elves are singing:
"Simm-simm-simmmm-
simm-simm-simmmm!"

Flying-flying-flying-flying,
swaying-swaying,
waving-waving-waving-waving,
weaving-weaving.

Tired from the roundalay,
to the blossom they fly away.

Flying-flying-flying-flying,
swaying-swaying
waving-waving-waving-waving,
weaving-weaving.

To the blossom they fly up,
slip into the blossom cup.
Inside the elves are resting too.
Soo-soo-soooo.

Text
1. From blossom cup they slip away -

2. the elves

3. join in a roundalay.

Gestures
1. The children and the teacher sit in a circle on stools, on pillows or on their knees on the floor. The teacher has hands on side of cheeks and head bowed. Now begin to speak very melodically while removing hands from cheeks and lifting head. Raise arms overhead while standing up. Give time for each movement.

2. Standing up, move loosely, outstretched arms as wings, down to horizontal position.

3. Staying with wing gesture, turn from waist up at the word "round," first a little to left and then to right.

4. They fly

↑ ↓

5. and hover,

6. They wave and

⌣➚

7. weave.

←→

8. Flying-flying-flying-flying,

↑ ↓ ↑ ↓

9. swaying-swaying,

⤹ ⤸

10. waving-waving-waving-waving,

11. weaving-weaving.

12. "Simmmm!"

13. There sounds a light ringing.

14. "Simmmm!"

15. The flower elves are singing:

  v   v

4. At "They fly," stay in place while moving wings up and down.

5. On the word "hover," lift onto toes while making a light upward movement with wings as if floating.

6. Standing once again on full foot, bring arms and hands loosely in front of shoulders with palms down and make a wave gesture toward the children.

7. At the end of the "wave" gesture, still standing, move hands parallel with palms down in a horizontal position, first to right then to left and then back to right. Speak slowly, stretching the word, and move gently.

8. Now begin with an easy, gliding walk, not too fast, moving freely around the room while loosely stretching arms out in a flying gesture.

9. While continuing to walk, keep arms in a floating gesture and lightly sway upper body from left to right.

10. Now continue walking around the room while moving arms in a wave gesture as in (6).

11. At "weaving," move arms as in (7) while continuing to walk. Then walk a few more steps in silence.

12. Now begin singing, "Simmmm!" in a light voice and gradually come to standing as you end the tone. Wait until everyone is standing still, then bring right hand to right ear in listening gesture.

13. After speaking these words, listen a little while more and sing again:

14. Let the "Simmmm!" quietly go before dissolving the listening gesture and turning to the children.

15. Nod in confirmation at each v.

16. "Simm - simm - simmmm-

Simm - simm - simmmm!"

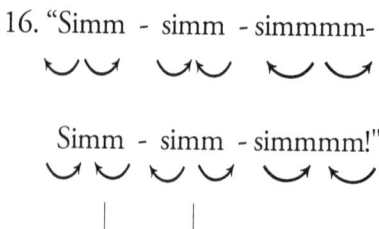

17. Flying-flying-flying-flying,
    swaying-swaying,
    waving-waving-waving-waving,
    weaving-weaving.

18. Tired from the roundalay,

19. to the blossom they fly away.

20. Flying-flying-flying-flying,
    swaying-swaying,
    waving-waving-waving-waving,
    weaving-weaving.

21. To the blossom they fly up,

22. slip into the blossom cup.

23. Inside the elves are resting too.

24. Soo - soo - soooo

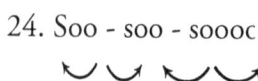

16. **With arms outstretched at chest height, palms facing children, make a loose swaying gesture with hands outward towards right and left for the first line and then the return gesture for the second line following direction of the arrows in text. Each time, let the third "Simmmm" quietly go.

17. Here, follow the movement sequence as described above (as in 8-11). Then after a few silent steps, gradually stop and stay standing.

18. Let arms sink and bow head. Your body gesture emphasizes sleepiness.

19. Bring both hands together depicting a blossom. Wrists are touching and fingers are pointing upward, lightly rounded showing a blossom cup.

20. Here follow the movement as above in (8-11).

21. Return to starting point, if possible, and remain standing (or stand in another place if necessary)

22. Now reverse the gesture as in (1) above.

23. And bow your head, which rests once again with hands on either side of cheeks, eventually lowering eyelids.

24. ***In this position rock slightly back and forth.

Notes

Consider the following for the movement game:
- Establish if there is enough space to move freely around the room
- If space is tight, then move clockwise in a circle direction, though not standing directly on a circle line.

**When the children know and trust the game, the teacher can bring a variation on the elves singing with finger cymbals which should be struck everytime "Simmmm" would have been sung. Take hold of cymbals firmly during silent walking and strike them instead of singing. After striking, bring the cymbals up overhead and continue outward in an arc gesture to stretch the sound while gradually coming to standing. Move the cymbals to your right ear and listen to the sound and say, "There sounds a light ringing." Strike the cymbals a second time, moving them again into an arc and let the sound stretch (eventually swing cymbals lightly back and forth).

At "The flower elves are singing," turn to the children with a confirming nod.

Handle the cymbals as follows: At each "Simm-simm," strike the left cymbal edge just slightly with the right cymbal, forward and back. At "Simmmm!" strike the cymbals again, moving them up into an arc gesture and repeat sequence.

After the sound ends, move to flying gesture with cymbals still in hand, and find a moment without breaking the gesture, to let the cymbals disappear into your bag.

***Here are various possibilities to close the circle game:

- Speak (almost singing) the "Soo-soo-sooo!" quietly.
- Hum, sing, or play a lullaby on the pentatonic choroi flute.
- Sing or play the "sleepy" song (see next page) on the Choroi flute.

Sleepy: Mood of the Fifth Song
(Gently falling asleep)

It may be that one stanza is enough for the children.

Text for multiple elves (or children):

Sleepy are the wee elves (children) dear,
slip into a blossom cup near.
Sleep until the morning comes,
sleeping as a soft wind hums.
Soo-soo-soo-soo!
In the blossom safely rest.
Soo-oo-soo-oo-soo-oo-soo!

Evening wind sings from aloft,
rocking the grasses so soft.
Soo-soo-soo-soo!
Wee elves (children) love to listen too,
What a lovely, sleepy sound,
Singing over grass and ground.
Mm-m-m-m-m-mm! Mm-mm-mmm!

The song can be repeated in one or more of the following ways to give the children a longer quiet time:
- Hum or sing (la-la la)
- Play on Choroi Kinderharp
- Play on Choroi Pentatonic Flute

The quality of tone of the Choroi instruments corresponds to the constitutional condition of the young child in the first seven years and also to that of children with special needs. The overtones and low resonance sound do not infringe upon the flexible physical organization, nor do they press upon the soul structure. The tone hovers in space and blows softly, stroking the child like a puff of air. If there are no Choroi instruments available, then singing is preferable. A bamboo flute or Kantele can serve as long as they are played very gently. The soprano block flute's direct and grounding tone is not appropriate for the young child's constitution.

To Be an Elf Child
A little rhythmical-musical story without gestures

Unseen beings who live and weave,
in every blossom cup you breathe,
You bright elves so tender and fine,
I wish you were play-mates of mine.

Hovering lightly I dance and sway,
flying with blossom wings, I pray,
in blossom rocked by wind so mild,
living with you like an elfin child.

At night, sleeping in bed I lie
I dream that like an elf I fly.
Hovering high over elfin ring,
deep in the blossom cup I swing.
Like the elves, I will help show
how every little bud can grow.

Joyfully, wakening with the sun,
laughing, into the garden (meadow, forest) I run
and say, "Thank you to all little beings
who visited me, in my dreams."

You bright elves so tender and fine,
oh to be an elf child of mine.

IN THE MOUNTAIN

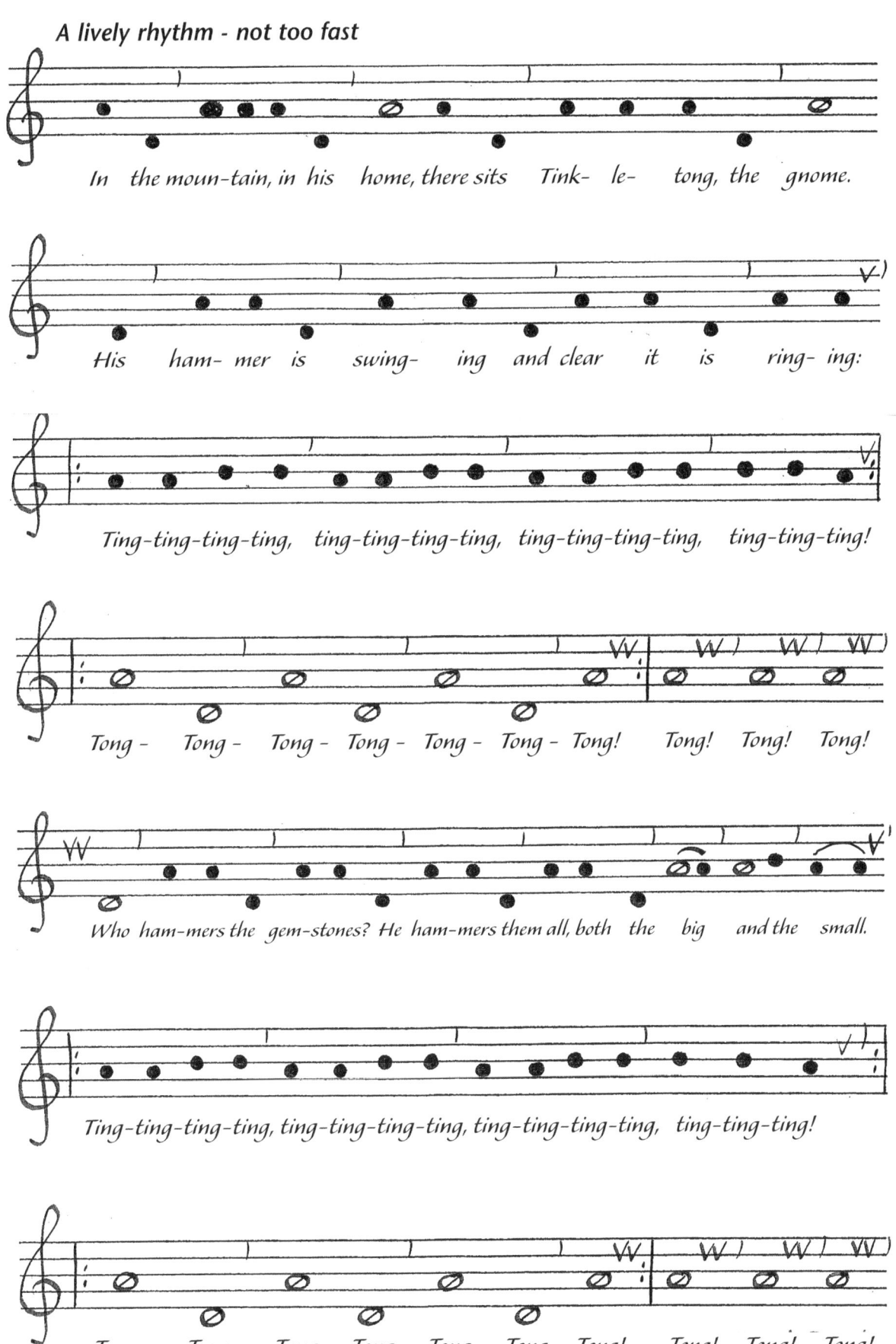

In the Mountain

A lively rhythm—not too fast

A

*In the mountain, in his home,
there sits Tinkletong, the gnome.
His hammer is swinging and clear it is ringing:
Ting-ting-ting-ting, ting-ting-ting-ting, ting-ting-ting-ting, ting-ting-ting!
Ting-ting-ting-ting, ting-ting-ting-ting, ting-ting-ting-ting, ting-ting-ting!*

*Tong - Tong - Tong - Tong - Tong - Tong - Tong - Tong - Tong - Tong - Tong - Tong - Tong - Tong!
Tong! Tong! Tong!*

B

*Who hammers the gemstones?
He hammers them all,
both the big and the small.
Ting-ting-ting-ting, ting-ting-ting-ting,
ting-ting-ting-ting, ting-ting-ting!
Ting-ting-ting-ting, ting-ting-ting-ting,
ting-ting-ting-ting, ting-ting-ting!*

*Tong - Tong - Tong - Tong - Tong - Tong - Tong - Tong - Tong - Tong - Tong - Tong - Tong - Tong!
Tong! Tong! Tong!*

Repeat Part A

A final stanza is spoken following the repeat of Part A:

Closing Verse:

*So hammers,
so hammers
the gnome
in his home.
He hammers big,
he hammers small
the precious gemstones all.*

A: Text

1. In the mountain, in his home,

2. there sits

3. Tinkletong, the gnome.
   X   X

4. His hammer is swinging and clear it is ringing:

5. Ting-ting-ting-ting, ting-ting-ting-ting,
ting-ting-ting-ting, ting-ting-ting!

Ting-ting-ting-ting, ting-ting-ting-ting,
ting-ting-ting-ting, ting-ting-ting!

6. Tong - Tong - Tong - Tong - Tong - Tong - Tong!
Tong - Tong - Tong - Tong - Tong - Tong - Tong!
Tong! Tong! Tong!

A: Gestures

1. While singing, bring hands from the side upwards in an arch above the head, at "mountain." When the word "home" is used, form a steep roof overhead with fingertips together.

2. Make a pointed hat with fingertips together and resting thumbs and wrist on forehead.

3. With the pointed hat on head, bow upper body forward at each "X".

4. With outstretched arm, swing right fist back and forth like a little hammer, as shown by the arrows under the text.

5. Now, also make a fist with the left hand. With the right fist, pinky side down, as the little hammer, gently knock according to the speech rhythm on the middle knuckle of the curled left index finger, the "little jewel."

6. Turn the whole left fist, pinky side down, to represent the "big jewel," and pound according to the speech rhythm, with great momentum.

B: Text

7. Who hammers the gemstones?

8. He hammers them all,
   ↓   ↓

9. both the big

10. and the small.

11. Ting-ting-ting-ting, ting-ting-ting-ting, ting-ting-ting-ting, ting-ting-ting! Ting-ting-ting-ting, ting-ting-ting-ting, ting-ting-ting-ting, ting-ting-ting!

12. Tong - Tong - Tong - Tong - Tong - Tong - Tong! Tong - Tong - Tong - Tong - Tong - Tong - Tong! Tong! Tong! Tong!

B: Gestures

7. With left hand at left ear, listen inside the mountain home.

8. Again, make two fists and hammer once on the jewel each time at the arrow.

9. With both hands show a "big jewel," as if holding a ball at chest height.

10. With left hand enclose the right fist as a "small jewel" on your right thigh.

11. Again, hammer as in 5.

12. Again, hammer as in 6.

Repeat Part A

Following this repeat, a closing verse is spoken:

Text

15. So hammers, so hammers,

16. the Gnome

17. in his home.

18. He hammers big,

19. he hammers small

20. the precious

21. gemstones all.

Gestures

15. Swing the little hammer as in 4.

16. Put on the pointed hat as in 2

17. And show the home as in 1.

18. Show the big jewel as in 9.

19. Show the little jewel as in 10.

20. At the word "precious" make a great arch with both hands and arms, moving from overhead out to the sides.

21. Bring the hands together again in front of you like two little bowls in which the jewels lie. Hold this gesture awhile.

Ending:

The hammering stops on the mountain floor.
The little fellow can't hammer one bit more.
So little Tinkletong, the gnome,
lays his hammer down.
In his mountain home, the gnome is resting now.
His tired eyes, he's closing now...

Text

1. The hammering stops on the mountain floor.

2. The little fellow can't hammer one bit more.

3. So little Tinkletong, the gnome, lays his hammer down.

4. In his mountain home, the gnome is resting now.

5. His tired eyes, he's closing now...

Gestures

1. Take your little hammer up high and hold it still.

2. At "can't hammer one bit more," shake your head.

3. Lay your little hammer with emphasis on your thigh or on the floor and dissolve the gesture.

4. Raise hands together over your head as "mountain."

5. At "tired," put both hands together and lay your left cheek on them or support head in both hands.

Quiet Fifth

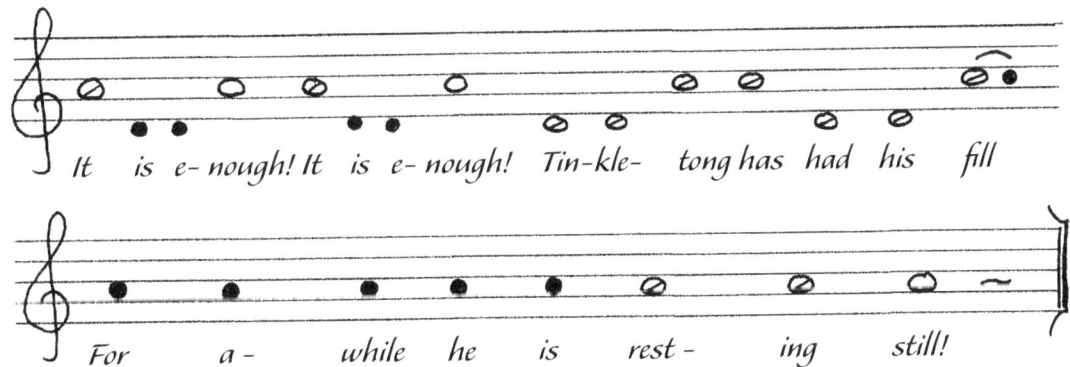

After the quiet fifth song is sung, the melody can be hummed. You can also just hum the song or play it on a pentatonic Choroi flute. On a Choroi interval flute the notes A and D can also be played.

We'll invite our flute to come,
and join us while we rest some.
There is nothing more to hear.
Tinkletong, the gnome,
is resting in his mountain home.

Text

1. We'll invite our flute to come,
and join us while we rest some.

2. There is nothing more to hear.

3. Tinkletong, the gnome,
is resting in his mountain home.

Gestures

1. The teacher holds the flute so it is very visible to the children and begins to play the melody of the Quiet-Diddledo very tenderly.

2. Bring right hand to right ear in listening gesture.

3. Clasp forearms together near forehead and lay head down upon them. Stay there a little while.

Quiet-Diddledo

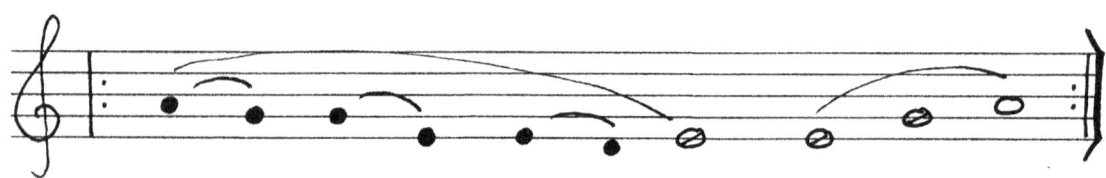

After resting, to repeat the game again:

Rested, rested,
Tinkletong has rested.
The little fellow begins once more,
To hammer on his mountain floor.

Text

1. Rested, rested,
Tinkletong has rested.

2. The little fellow begins once more,

3. to hammer on his mountain floor.

Gestures

1. At the words "Rested - rested", stretch arms in waking gesture.

2. At "little fellow" show once more the pointed cap.

3. Make a fist with the right hand as the little hammer, stretch right arm high, and swing back and forth according to the arrows. Then the game starts over from the beginning.

IN WOODLAND A SOFT CRACK!
A little hand-gesture story

Crick - - and crack - - !
Crick de crick and crack de crack.
In woodland a soft crack!
Crick de crick and crack de crack.
Just listen to it smack!

Crick de crick and crack de crack.
Listen: crick! A twig cracks quick!
Crick de crick and crack de crack.
A gnome: he steps on it.

Crick de crick and crack de crack.
With his heavy pack -
crick de crick and crack de crack -
he wanders on the track.

Crick de crick and crack de crack.
Crick de crick and crack de crack.
And crick - - and crack.
Crick - - - - crack.
-- Listen! --
No! It cracks no more.
The woodland gnome with heavy pack
wanders not as once before.
He sits up in his mountain keep
and there he rests,
and goes to sleep.

This game is a hand gesture game that can also be played on wooden sticks. In the hand gesture game, the word "crick" will be emphasized by tapping the index fingers together, crossing near the tips, and at the word "crack" crossing the index fingers at the middle.

You can proceed similarly with the wooden sticks: Tap the stick ends at "crick" and tap the stick middles at "crack." If you also tap lightly at the ends and firmly at the middle, you will create a differentiated brighter sound, similar to the vowels "i" and "a." Because the text is identical for the hand gesture game and the sticks, you will find the directions for using the sticks (indicated with "a") under the numbered hand gesture directions.

Text	**Gestures**
1. Crick - and crack - ! ○ ●	1. For the word "crick" (○) tap left pointer with tip of right pointer, using top segments of fingers. For the word "crack" (●) use middle segment of fingers. a. Firmly strike the tip of the left stick with the tip of the right stick for "crick" (○). Lightly strike the middle of the left stick with the middle of the right stick for "crack" (●).
2. Crick de crick and crack de crack. ○ ○ ● ●	2. Repeat as above, twice each, speaking with strong rhythmic accent: "crick" in high voice, "crack" in lower voice. a. At every ○ lightly tap stick tips and at every ● firmly tap stick middles.
3. In woodland a soft crack! ●	3. Bring right hand against right ear, listening. Speak mysteriously. a. Lift the right stick vertically as if listening attentively. At "crack" tap the sticks together at the middle.
4. Crick de crick and crack de crack. ○ ○ ● ●	4. See above as in 2. a. See above as in 2a.
5. Just listen to it smack! ●	5. For the word "listen" bring right hand once again to right ear and at "smack" strike the middle of the left pointer finger again with the middle of the right pointer finger. a. For the word "listen" lift the right stick vertically as if listening attentively as in 3a. At "smack" tap the sticks together at the middle.
6. Crick de crick and crack de crack. ○ ○ ● ●	6. See above as in 2. a. See above as in 2a.
7. Listen: crick! ○	7. For the word "listen" bring right hand once again to right ear and at "crick," tap the tip of left pointer finger again with the tip of the right pointer finger. a. For the word "listen" lift the the right stick vertically as if listening attentively as in 3a. At "crick," tap the tip of the left stick again with the tip of the right stick.

8. A twig cracks quick!

8. Hold both pointers horizontally, points touching to form a "twig." The other fingers are rolled in toward the palm. At "cracks," drop both pointer fingertips down; the twig is broken.
a. Push the tips of the sticks against each other, making a horizontal "twig." At "cracks," let the tips drop down to point to the ground; the twig is broken.

9. Crick de crick and crack de crack.
    ○   ○   ●   ●

9. See above as in 2.
a. See above as in 2a.

10. A gnome:

10. Show right fist with thumb laying on outside of rolled fingers, the back of hand facing self. The pinky finger sticks vertically up as the "gnome". Say the word "Gnome" in a bright voice.
a. At "gnome" tap the vertically-held right stick on the horizontally-held left stick and then spring it back up.

11. he steps on it.

11. With right pinkie held vertically downward, poke thigh.
a. At "steps," strike the vertically-held right stick on the horizontally-held left stick with force, emphasizing the "e" in "steps."

12. Crick de crick and crack de crack.
    ○   ○   ●   ●

12. See above as in 2.
a. See above as in 2a.

13. With his heavy pack -

13. With both fists at the right of your neck, pretend to hold a little sack, leaning slightly forward to show a heavy weight.
a. Making of the two sticks a little "sack," on the word "with" heave them up to the right shoulder. On the word "heavy" lean slightly forward.

14 crick de crick and crack de crack -
    ○   ○   ●   ●

14. See above as in 2.
a. See above as in 2a.

15. he wanders on the track.

15. With right pointer held vertically downward, tap thigh heading towards knee on the stressed syllables.
a. Hold the right stick vertically and poke with the lower end on the horizontally-held left stick, from the middle toward the tip, on the stressed syllables.

16. Crick de crick and crack de crack.
     o   o   •   •

Crick de crick and crack de crack.
  o   o   •   •

16. See above as in 2, twice.
a. See above as in 2a, twice.

17. And crick - and crack.
      o   •

17. Do the hand gestures as always, but after "crick" and "crack" pause to listen a little longer.
a. Do the stick movements as always, but after "crick" and "crack" pause to listen a little longer.

18. Crick - crack.
    o   •

18 Tap as always on "crick," and listen a bit longer. Then tap on "crack" and listen for a long time, holding the pointer finger very still.
a. Tap sticks as always on "crick," and listen a bit longer. Then tap on "crack" and listen for a long time, holding the stick very still.

19. - Listen! -

19. Bring right hand to right ear and listen.
a. Lift right stick up as in 3a above and hold it in a listening gesture a while.

20. No! It cracks no more.
    ←   →   ←

20. Say "No" in a confirming way and shake head.
a. Hold both sticks vertically and move them in a "no" gesture, saying a confirming "no."

21. The woodland dwarf with heavy pack
       ↶   ↓

21. See above as in 13.
a. See above as in 13a.

22. wanders not as once before.
       ←   →

22. Smile at the children and shake head.
a. Smile at the children and shake head.

23. He sits up in his mountain keep

24. and there he rests,

25. and goes to sleep.

23. Now bring arms out and up overhead into an arc until finger tips touch.
a. Now bring arms out and up overhead into an arc with stick tips touching as "mountain."

24. Bring arms down and wrap them around each other at the chest.
a. Bring the sticks down and lay them on your thighs.

25. Rest left cheek on joined palms, sleeping gesture.
a. Sitting in this position gently rock back and forth while the sticks remain on the thighs. When the game is done, lay the sticks carefully together without a sound.

At this point the closing verse can be inserted.

Closing verse
The woodland gnome is quiet now.
He closes his eyes, his head he bows.
Outside through the trees, the wind does blow:
Soft and low, soft and low.

Text
1. The woodland gnome is quiet now.

2. He closes his eyes, his head he bows.

3. Outside through the trees, the wind does blow: Soft and low, soft and low.

Gestures
1. Speak in a soft voice, keeping a quiet attitude for the entire ending.

2. Close eyes and lower head slightly.

3. Listening, with closed eyes, speak softly, very melodically, almost singing and with wonder: "Outside…the wind…" At "soft and low," begin to rock back and forth ever so slightly and keep rocking until the song ends.

The sticks can be made out of a soft wood like spruce. You can search for small sticks or branches with the children in the woods. Then they can pull the bark off and sand until the sticks are smooth. The sticks should be about 8" long.

You can also find wooden dowels in a hardware store that will work for sticks. Choose dowels that measure between 3/8 and 5/8 inches in diameter. Saw these rods into 8-inch pieces and sand the ends so they feel soft and round. Please do not use hardwood, so that the sensitive constitution of the young pre-school child is protected and not damaged. The same applies to the child with disabilities.

Recommendation

The game can end here, but it is advisable to end with the following lullaby, "The Wind Blows Through The Trees," so that the rhyming element is complemented by the melodic element.

THE WIND BLOWS THROUGH THE TREES

The song should always be tuned to the A tone as indicated. Sing freely following the language. Let the last "soo!" end peacefully. You can add the words, "Thank you, dear wind!" and bring arms down to the side, bowing lightly.

At "thank you," if the game is to transition into a movement game, then the "Pixie Dance" would be very suitable here. For this, remain sitting in the lullaby position, listen for awhile, and finally lay cheek upon your hands which are together with palms touching and say:

He sleeps and dreams, the pixie child.
He sleeps and dreams all through the night.
At dawn he wakes up, bright,
and from his mountain home
runs the pixie-gnome: tip-tip, tap-tap, tip-tip-tap,
down to the waiting meadow.

Text

1. He sleeps and dreams, the pixie child.
He sleeps and dreams all through the night.

2. At dawn he wakes up, bright,

3. and from his mountain home

4. runs the pixie-gnome:
tip-tip, tap-tap, tip-tip, tap,
 ⁔   ⁔   ⁔   ⁔   ⁔   ⁔   ⁔

5. down to the waiting meadow.

Gestures

1. Lay the left cheek on outside of hands, palms together in resting pose and speak softly.

2. Straighten body up and rub eyes

3. Raise hands over head, fingertips touching to indicate "mountain."

4. Tap right thigh with pointer fingertips, "running" toward the knee in the syllable rhythm as indicated by "⁔".

5. At "meadow" spread arms and hands out with palms facing down to suggest a meadow. Then follow with the "Pixie Dance."

THE PIXIE DANCE
Spatial movement game with hand gestures

'Twixt the grasses, shining new,
spider webs hang full of dew.
And it glitters, everywhere,
in the sunlight, crystal clear:
glitz - glitz - glitz - glitz.

In the early light of day,
pixies dance the round-a-lay.
Walk in circle round about - round about,
always, always round-about.

Stopping. So! Turning slow
on their toes: tippy-toe.
Soft and light on their toes,
tippy-toe,
tippy - tippy - tippy -toe!

All are stopping, stopping slow:
bow their heads, low - low.
And their feet, they show - show:
tap - the right, tip - the left,
tap - the right, tip - the left.

Wave with both their hands: bye - bye.
Lalla-lalla-lalla-lie,
lalla-lalla-lalla-lie,
Oh, so fun, see just see.
Lala-lalla-lalla-lee!
Lala-lalla-lalla-lee!
Bend their heads again: low - low.
Dance round-a-round the ring: so - so.
Walk in circle round-about,
always, always round-about.
Stop! Stop now! Down they sit,
resting from the dance a bit.
All the pixies rest now too.
Soo - soo - soooo.

Text

1. 'Twixt the grasses, shining new,

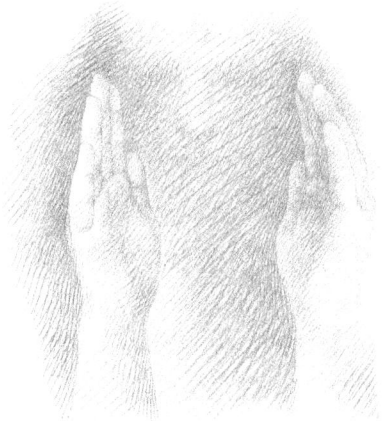

2. spider webs

3. hang full of dew.

Gestures

1. Hold lower arms and hands upright, fingers relaxed. At "grasses" stretch fingers (pointed grasses).

2. Hold hands at waist height, fingers spread out, palms down, middle fingers touching: "spider webs"

3. Loosen middle fingers. Both hands form "dew drops". Loosely roll in fingers, pointer and middle finger tips touch thumb. A hollow space remains (air). Move slowly, letting elbows sink down. (Dew drops hang.)

4.

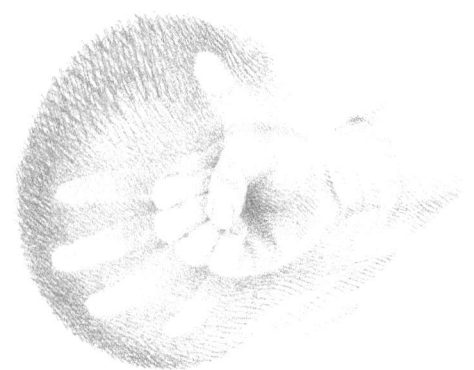

4. The sudden flaring up and disappearing of light is indicated by, in turn, opening the hands with spread fingers toward the front and then rolling them together again rhythmically (palms forward).

a. And it glitters, everywhere,
        r   l

b. in the sunlight, crystal clear:
       r   l

c. glitz - glitz -
   r   l

d. glitz - glitz.
   r   l

a. Right hand forward, left hand forward (chest height).
b. Right hand up (sun, above head), left hand forward (chest height)

c. Right hand further forward, toward the right (chest height), left hand further forward toward the left (chest height).

d. Right hand further forward, in the middle (stomach height), left hand further forward, in the middle (stomach height). The palm must be visible toward the front on "glitz." The center of the palm rays out.

5. In the early light of day,
pixies dance the round-a-lay.

5. Rise, inviting children with outstretched arms to form a ring, already circling "sunwise" (clockwise).

6. Walk in circle round about, round about, always, always round-about.

6. Continue circling until all are holding hands and the ring is complete. Continue circling a while. 5 and 6 may be repeated.

7. Stopping. So!

7. Stop, not abruptly but gradually. Prepare well. Face the center.

8. Turning slow

8. Lift both hands, sticking out pointers as if to say: "Attention!"

9. on their toes:

9. Slowly rise to toes. The knees remain loose.

10. tippy-toe.

11. Soft and light on their toes,

12. tippy - toe,
tippy- tippy- tippy-toe!

13. All are stopping, stopping slow:

14. bow their heads, low - low
                          v   v

15. And their feet, they show - show:
tap - the right, tip - the left,
tap - the right, tip - the left.

16. Wave with both their hands: bye - bye.
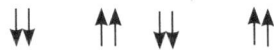

17. Lalla-lalla-lalla-lie,
lalla-lalla-lalla-lie,

18. Oh, so fun, see just see.

19. Lala-lalla-lalla-lee!
Lala-lalla-lalla-lee!

20. Bend their heads again: low - low.

10. In place, turn around right shoulder with many small steps. Keep knees loose.

11. Continue turning on tiptoes in small steps, hands as in 8. This helps with balance.

12. Half way around. Continue turning around right shoulder until facing center again. Movement is cautious and quiet, stepping freely, not bound by speech rhythm.

13. Face turned to center, drop back on your soles, lower hands.

14. At "low - low", nod two times.

15. Clearly shift weight to the left, touching the floor with top of right foot. Do the same with tip of left foot. Allow yourself time. This weight shifting is hard for young children. If they don't touch the floor in the right rhythm, or do it twice with the same foot or with the "wrong" foot, leave them be. Older children will quickly learn by repetition, don't correct them.

16. Lift arms and hands and wave hands down and up, in speech rhythm as shown.

17. Keep hands relaxed and lightly wave them freely and quickly up and down, moving a little to and fro, at head height.

18. Stop movement: hands forward, above head. Look up to hands, then move them slowly up and down, in rhythm.

19. As in 17. From 17 to 19 tiny movements, primarily with fingers.

20. Hands down. Then as in 14.

21. Dance round-a-round the ring: so - so.
Walk in circle round-about,
always, always round-about.

21. Open arms and hands in an invitation to hold hands while walking in a circle "sunwise," as in 6. (If necessary, repeat text.) If holding hands creates problems, walk behind each other, right shoulder to center.

22. Stop! Stop now!

22. As in 7.

23. Down they sit,

23. Return to stool and sit down.

24. resting from the dance a bit.

24. Prop up elbows, resting head in hands, or encircle head with arms and rest forehead on arms. Pause for rest.

Conclusion

25. All the pixies rest now too.
Soo - soo - soooo.
Or: I sing (or play) a lullaby for you.
Or: I sing (or play) the Quiet Diddledoo.

25. Speak these lines quietly to children, then sing the Quiet Diddledoo song below. Repeat with humming, or play on pentatonic Choroi flute.

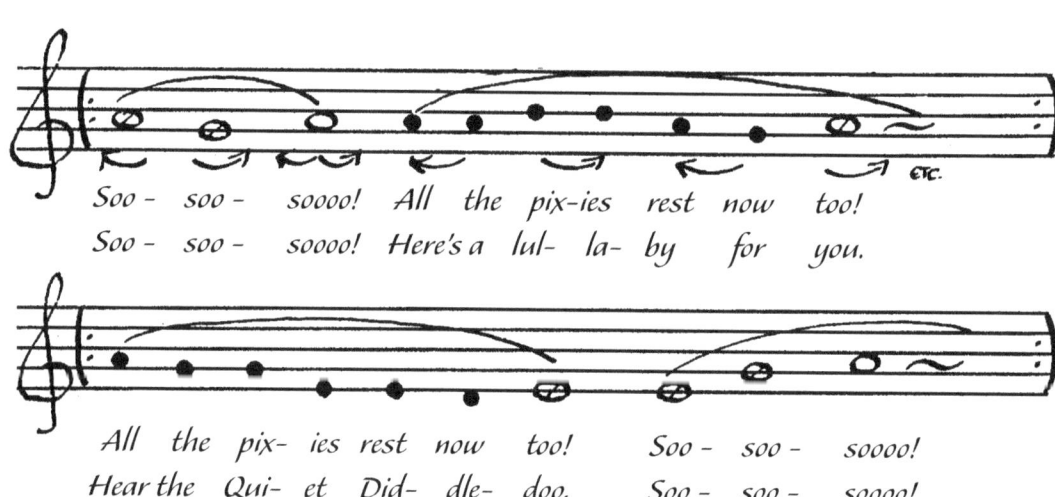

THE PIXIE DANCE (UNDER THE SPIDERWEB TENT)
Little story without gestures

'Twixt the grasses, shining new,
Spider webs hang full of dew.
How the early sunlight here
Shines like pearly dew, so clear!
And it glitters - here and there
Looks like crystals everywhere!

Under the spiderweb, glittering grand
Lives a secret fairyland!

Beetles rumble - beetles hum,
Hum a strange, amazing way
And the pixies turn around
In their circle round-a-lay.
Soom - soom - soomm, soom - soom - soomm,
Round-a, round-a-ring they come,
Tippy - tippy - tippy - toes,
Soft and light on their toes.

Heads bow down - feet, they show,
Tap - the right, tip - the left,
Wave with both their hands: bye - bye,
Lalla - lalla - lalla - lie.
Oh, how fun - see just see!

Heads bow, and in a round-a-lay
soom - soom - soomm, soom - soom - soomm,
round and round they make their way,
tippy - tippy - tippy - toes,
Soft and light on their toes.

With looking eyes- you'll see it!
With listening ears- you'll hear it!

Psst, I pray you, quiet all!
Don't disturb the pixies small!

Scoot
Rhythmic-musical hand and body gesture game
Also suitable as a spatial movement game

Under the root
lives the gnome Scoot.
The gnome, he loves the children true,
and the children love him too!

All around the ring they go.
Diddledoom – diddledoom – diddlediddlediddledoom.
He gently nods his head just so.
Dee-da-daa! Dee-da-daa!

When the children gaily sing –
lallala – lallala – lalla lalla lalla la –
he listens to the joyful ring.

Ha – ha – ha – haa! -- Ha – ha – ha – haa!
The children laugh, around jumps he.
Hopsa – hopsa – hopsassa!
Jumps and jumps, he's full of glee –
full of glee – full of glee –
jumping, jumping full of glee.

The children rest upon the moss.
Quietly 'round the gnome does sneak.
At sleeping faces he takes a peek.

If a child blinks or stirs near Scoot,
quick! He jumps under the root!
When the children go home again
he stays alone, gazing after them.

At night, when Scoot lies under the tree,
oh, what a wondrous dream has he!

With the children in a round
he bows to the sound: dee-da-daa-dee-da-daa.

Hears the singing,
hears the ringing: lallalaa – lallalaa.
At night he's not alone awhile.
He dreams – and in his dream he gently smiles!
The gnome, he loves the children true,
and the children love him, too!

Text

1. Under the root lives the gnome Scoot.

2. The gnome, he loves the children true,

Gestures

1. Cross arms in front of forehead, hands hanging down (as roots). At "Scoot" lift head with the crossed arms, looking out below them.

2. Spread arms forward, palms up, as if to give something.

3. and the children love him too!

4. All around the ring they go.
    r   l   r   l
Diddledoom-diddledoom-diddlediddlediddledoom.
  r   l   r   l   r   l   r   l

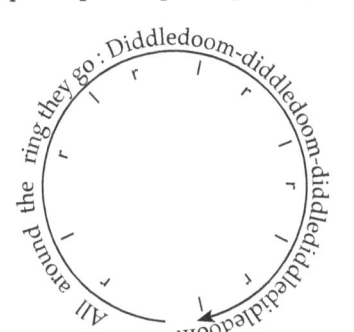

3. Caress your own cheek

4. Now "dance" the fingertips of both hands on thighs or the floor, going around in a clockwise direction, alternating right and left hand according to the (r, l) notations.

5. He gently nods his head just so.
          v   v
Dee - da - daa! dee - da - daa!
 v   v   v   v

5. At every "v" gently nod head.

6. When the children gaily   sing -

lallala - lallala - lalla lalla lalla la -

Movement rhythm:

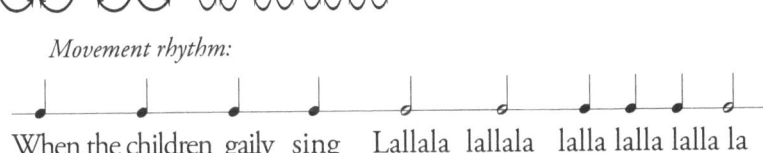

When the children gaily sing Lallala lallala lalla lalla lalla la

6. Speak the "lallala" very melodically and make light, airy conducting movements along with it. Begin at chest level, with an upward movement. Stretch out the last "la" somewhat.

7. He listens to the joyful ring.

7. Put both hands behind the ears and listen for a while.

8. Ha-ha ha-haa! Ha-ha-ha-haa!
   o   o o   o

8. Raise arms to each side above head (see illustration) and loosely turn hands out and in. If playing while kneeling on the floor, rise to an erect kneeling position for the laugh, and return to a sitting kneeling position for the next line of text.

9. The children laugh,
      x   x

9. Clap hands softly, light as air, at each "*x*". After the second clap bring hands down in a large arc over the outside.

10. around jumps he.
    ↑r   ↑l

Hopsa - hopsa - hopsassa!
↑r   ↑l   ↑r ↑l

Jumps and jumps, he's full of glee.
↑r   ↑r   ↑l   – –

10. Make hands into fists and let them "bounce" alternately with the edge of the little finger on the thighs or the floor. At "glee" put both fists next to each other on thighs or floor.

11. Full of glee - full of glee -
    o o o o   o o o o

jumping, jumping full of glee.
   o   o   o   o

11. Bring hands up to sides slightly above head height and turn hands out and in loosely at each " o ". For the second line of text, rise to an upright kneeling position, if game is being performed on the floor.

12. (Silent movement)

12. Lower hands either to thighs or floor, and if kneeling upright, return to a sitting kneeling position.

13. The children rest upon the moss.

13. Let hands rest loosely, and slowly tilt head. Remain sitting like this for a while.

14. Quietly 'round the gnome does sneak,
    r   l   r   l   r   l   r

14. With pointer fingertips, tap right and left finger alternately on thigh, moving from hip to knee forward, or if on the floor, from close to the body forward.

15. At sleeping faces he takes a peek.

15. Put both hands to forehead as a "shield" and look out from underneath. Then take the hands down and put them on the thighs.

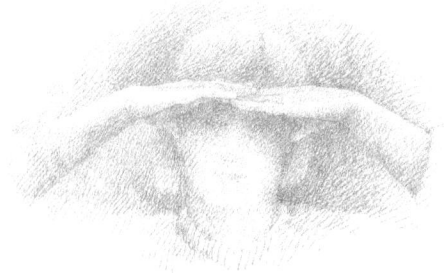

16. If a child blinks or stirs near Scoot,

16. At "blinks" squint eyes, at "stirs" waggle head slightly back and forth.

17. quick! He jumps

18. under the root!

19. When the children go home again

20. he stays alone,

21. gazing after them.

22. (Silent gesture)

23. At night, when Scoot lies under the tree,

24. oh, what a wondrous dream has he!

17. Suddenly raise arms.

18. Cross the forearms in front of the forehead, as above in 1.

- Pause -

19. At "home" point both hands forward.

20. Place both hands flat upon the chest.

21. Put both hands to forehead again as a shield and look after the departing children for a while, leaning the upper body slightly forward.

22. Move the upper body back and place the hands again flat upon the chest.

23. Spread arms and hands sideways and upward, as branches of a tree. Do not overstretch the arms. If on the ground, rise with the "tree" into an upright kneeling position.

24. Put hands to cheeks and support head. Lower eyelids, so as to still see the floor. If in an upright kneeling position, go back to a sitting kneeling position.

25. With the children in a round,

he bows to the sound:

Dee - da - daa - dee - da - daa.
  ᵥ   ᵥ   ᵥ   ᵥ

26. Hears the singing,

27. hears the ringing:

28. lallalaa - lallalaa.

29. At night he's not alone awhile.

30. He dreams -

31. and in his dream he gently smiles!

32. The gnome, he loves the children true, and the children love him, too!

25. Speak quieter and slower, almost singing, swaying upper body back and forth very slightly, almost imperceptibly (see arrows).

At ᵥ nod slightly.

26. Take hands away from cheeks.

27. Put hands behind ears and listen.

28. Accompany dreamy-sounding singing with very small, only implied conducting movements (see above at 6).

29. On the word "night" put fingertips together and place them on head as a pointed cap. On "not alone," turn head a little to left and right.

30. Put hands to cheeks and support head. Lower eyelids, so as to still see the floor. (See above as at 24.)

31. Raise head with hands still on cheeks. With a slight smile, speak, almost singing: "he gently smiles." Continue to hold this position for a while with slightly open, smiling mouth and lowered eyelids.

32. Gestures as above in 2 and 3, but since the gnome is dreaming, perform all with closed eyelids.

Note
The game can end here.

Alternatively, a nice complement to round off the game is "Scoot's Dream Song" ("The Wind Blows Through the Trees"). It can be sung without hand gestures. Singing without hand gestures is quite special, like a parent taking their child on their lap and rocking gently back and forth while singing.

If singing with hand gestures, introduce the song as follows:

33. The wind brings him a dream.	33. Lay hands on cheeks and assume the dream gesture (as above in 24), then beckon the wind to you with both hands.

In the Autumn, during lantern festival time, the "Scoot" game can be followed by the farewell game, "What Scoot does in Wintertime" (see p. 64).

In the early part of the year, the game "The Root Gnome" (see p. 14) can connect the children to the living and weaving of the elemental beings as they come back up to earth.

Scoot's Dream Song
("The Wind Blows Through the Trees")

The wind blows through the trees,
brings dreams along the breeze.
Soo-oo, soo-oo, soo-oo, soo!
So soft and fine he sings,
sweet dreams to them he brings.
Soo-oo, soo-oo, soo-oo, soo!
Soo-oo, soo-oo, soo-oo, soo!

The quiet evening wind so mild---
also rocks the root child.
Soo-oo, soo-oo, soo-oo, soo!
And just as with the trees,
come dreams along the breeze.
Soo-oo, soo-oo, soo-oo, soo!
Soo-oo, soo-oo, soo-oo, soo!

And underneath his root
the little gnome, Scoot,
soo-oo, soo-oo, soo-oo, soo!
In the middle of the night
laughed softly with delight.
Mm, mm-m, mm-m, mmmm-
Mm, mm-m, mm-m, mmmm-!
Mm-mm-mmm.

Text

1. The wind blows through the trees,

2. Brings dreams along the breeze.

3. Soo-oo, soo-oo, soo-oo, soo!

4. So soft and fine he sings,

5. sweet dreams to them he brings.
   Soo-oo, soo-oo, soo-oo, soo!

   Soo-oo, soo-oo, soo-oo, soo!

6. The quiet evening wind so mild---

Gestures

1. With both hands wave the "wind" towards you at the words "wind" and then "trees."

2. Then go into the dream gesture: lay hands on each cheek supporting head, lower eyelids so you can still see the floor and smile.

3. In rocking rhythm following the arrow directions, rock the head, still resting in hands, lightly back and forth.

4. Now take hands from cheeks and spread arms up and out to the side, slightly bent, to form "boughs."

5. Continue rocking the upper body slightly back and forth while in the "tree gesture."

6. As above in 1.

7. also rocks the root child.

8. Soo-oo, soo-oo, soo-oo, soo!

9. And just as with the trees,

10. come dreams along the breeze.

11. Soo-oo, soo-oo, soo-oo, soo!
    Soo-oo, soo-oo, soo-oo, soo!

12. And underneath his root

13. the little gnome, Scoot,
    ↓   ↑

14. Soo-oo, soo-oo, soo-oo, soo!

15. In the middle of the night

16. laughed softly with delight.

17. Mm, mm-m, mm-m, mmmm-
    Mm, mm-m, mm-m, mmmm-!

18. Mm-mm-mmm

7. Bow head slightly and lay forearms across each other at forehead, with wrists and fingers hanging down loosely as the "roots."

8. As above in 3.

9. Make "tree gesture" as above in 4.

10. And here make the "dream gesture" as above in 2.

11. Refer above to 3.

12. Refer above to 7.

13. Leave the arms by the forehead and at "little" bow head and at "Scoot" raise head.

14. Keeping the gesture as described in 7, rock gently back and forth.

15. Now bring the arms down from forehead, forming a small arch in front of you, until the palms reach the floor. Bow head slightly.

16. Slowly lift hands and head forming the "dream gesture" as described above in 2.

17. Rock back and forth as above in 3.

18. Stay sitting quietly in the "dream gesture". Smile and hum, ever more slowly and quietly. After the tone has faded, bow head slowly and stay sitting a while longer.

Note

This song with gestures can be added to the hand gesture game to become the ending, either as a song with gestures that all participate in or as a song that is sung alone for rest time. The children can sit on a stool or lie on the floor, while the teacher, also in resting position, sings gently and quietly to the children. You can also sing while going around and stroking the head and back of each child. You can intuit what is right for the group. In a parent-child class, the parents can rock or stroke their children.

*Softly laughs Scoot
under the root ...*

Wilma Ellersiek.

WHAT SCOOT DOES IN WINTERTIME
Rhythmic-musical hand gesture game

There is a story I must tell.
Listen, listen to it well.
When we journey in the wood
we will no longer visit Scoot!
For it is empty, under his root.

Scoot has slipped into the ground.
Not alone, he can be found,
among the onions and tubers all,
and the roots both big and small.
He cares for the roots and he makes them strong
down below the whole winter long.

Then, comes the springtime sun--
it shines upon the earth.
Out comes the root gnome once again.
Under the root lives little Scoot.

Then to him we shall be springing-springing,
with dancing, talking, and with singing-singing.
Again, joy to him we will be bringing.
Yes! Joy we will be bringing.

Text
1. There is a story I must tell.
    v

2. Listen, listen to it well.

3. When we journey in the wood

4. we will no longer visit Scoot!
   ←—— ——→

Gestures
1. Sitting on a stool or on knees on the floor, invite the children to gather and nod at the word, "must."

2. At the word "listen," place hands at ears.

3. At the word "wood" lift arms and hands with fingers spread as trees. Rise to upright kneeling stance.

4. Lay both hands flat on the thighs and shake head once back and forth on "will no longer." At the word, "Scoot," show a pointed hat (see picture) on your head. Move back to sitting on knees.

5. For it is empty, under his root.

6. Scoot has slipped

7. into the ground.

8. Not alone, he can be found,
   ← →

9. among the onions

10. and tubers all,

11. and the roots both big and small.

5. At "empty," show empty hands, right and left, at each side of thighs. Then, at "root," lay forehead on crossed forearms, letting hands hang down.

6. At "Scoot," show a pointed hat on your head once more and gently bend forward, far enough that the point of the hat arrives at your knees.

7. Straighten yourself back up at "ground," and indicate the earth's surface with arms resting on the ground. You can push on the ground.

8. Shake head "no" and point downward with both hands.

9. Now make two fists resting side by side on thighs to represent "onions."

10. For "tubers," lay fists close to each other on knees with thumbs pointed up to form a fat tuber.

11. For the "big roots," cross forearms and rest on knees while letting the hands hang over the knees, with fingers lightly spread. For the "small roots," uncross forearms and lay them on thighs with wrists directly on knees, while each hand hangs down separately.

12. He cares for the roots
    T   I   M   R   P

12. Let the left hand remain hanging and enclose each finger of the left hand with the fingertips of the right hand, slowly caressing downward as if cleaning the little roots, one after the other beginning with thumb. (*T*=thumb, *I*=index finger, *M*=middle finger, *R*=ring finger, *P*=pinky).

13. and he makes them strong
    T   I   M   R   P

13. Make the same gesture as in 12, but switch hands.

14. down below

14. Now, holding the hands flat, side-by-side with palms down, move them slowly downward until you touch your knees with your finger "roots," indicating the earth's surface.

15. the whole winter long.
    ← → →←

15. Move hands horizontally as the arrows show, apart and together. This gesture is a gentle, protecting stroke like covering with a blanket.

16. Then, comes the springtime sun—

16. Make soft fists with both hands touching at thumbs and lay them on knees. The arms are rounded wide as if encircling a large ball. In this position, raise the arms slowly and at about chest height, open the fingers like sun rays. Raise rounded arms even higher until the hands slant towards the forehead.

17. it shines upon the earth.

17. Bow so the sun gesture inclines slightly forward. After speaking text, bow a little further forward, to show the warmth of the sunlight.

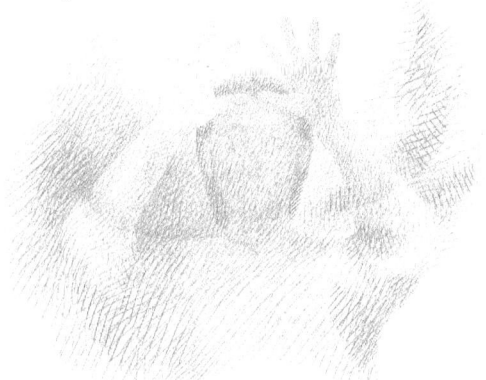

18. Out comes the root gnome once again.

18. At "root gnome," put your pointed hat back on as seen in 4. After "once again," silently place hands with palms facing upwards beside the knees and bend upper body forward, then straighten up, raising hands at the same time so that they are parallel.

19. Under the root

19. Without interruption, let hands and arms cross at bowed forehead in root gesture as in 5.

20. lives little Scoot.

20. When the word, "Scoot," is spoken, raise arms and hands up so that face appears, keeping root gesture.

21. Then to him we shall be springing - springing,
↑l   ↑r

21. Lower arms into a welcoming gesture, from outward on the side to front and center. At the word, "him," point with both hands to an imaginary figure in front of you. At, "springing," let alternating fists jump lightly off thighs and then "spring" towards knees.

22. with dancing, talking, and with singing - singing.
   o   o   o   ‿‿ ‿‿

22. Here, raise arms and hands and turn the hands in and out in the indicated speech rhythm. Make conducting movements to both "singing" words. If sitting on the floor, rise to a kneeling position for this line.

23. Again, joy to him we will be bringing.
    X   X   X   X

23. At X, clap hands quietly and lightly in a circular motion.

24. Yes! Joy we will be bringing.
        X

24. Say the word "Yes" with a quiet nod. After clapping on "Joy," raise hands up and outward in a great arch overhead and then lay them in lap as you sit back down.

67

WHO TROMPS AROUND ALL THROUGH THE WOOD?
Rhythmic-musical hand game for two fists

Rom and rum! - Rom and rum!
Rom and rum and rom and rum!
Who tromps around through all the wood?
It is the G I A N T Rommelgood!

Rom and rum! - Rom and rum!
Rom and rum and rom and rum!
So tromps the G I A N T of a man
with G I A N T steps across the land.

Rom and rum! - Rom and rum!
Rom and rum and rom and rum!
He is as tall as any tree.
Aloft, his head you hardly see.

Rom and rum! - Rom and rum!
Rom and rum and rom and rum!
But his tremendous, G I A N T hat,
you can see that, you can see that!

Rom and rum! - Rom and rum!
Rom and rum and rom and rum!
Who tromps around through all the wood?
It is the G I A N T Rommelgood!

Rom and rum! - Rom and rum!
Rom and rum and rom and rum!

Text: Speech must be formed so that gesture and sound are experienced rhythmically and musically. In your speech, contrast the rhythmic-accented tromping movements with the more melodic "calling" portions.
Gestures: Prepare gestures well before speaking, so that speech always coincides with the gesture. Make both hands into fists, the thumb on top of the rolled-in pointer. Set fists firmly on thighs, first right and then left (the rolled in fingers pointing down). Keep relaxed in hand and wrist. The Giant's steps are heavy, big, not loud; he tromps, not stomps.

Text
1. Rom and rum! Rom and rum!

Rom and rum and rom and rum!

Who tromps around through all the wood?

Gestures
1. When "tromping" with fists, accent the "m" in "Rommm" & "rummm." Continue tromps on accented syllables (indicated with ___) until "wood." Swing along with upper body.

2. It is the GIANT Rommelgood!

2. Stretch arms up with clenched fists. Stretch the upper body too. Speak slowly, almost calling!

3. Rom and rum! - Rom and rum!
Rom and rum and rom and rum!

3. Tromping as in 1.

4. So tromps the G I A N T of a man

4. On "tromps" press both fists together on thighs. On "giant of a man," stretch as in 2.

5. with G I A N T steps across the land.
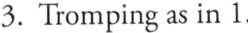

5. Simultaneously one arm moves down and the other moves up with both fists clenched. At "land" lift both arms up. Stretch out speech.

6. Rom and rum! - Rom and rum!
Rom and rum and rom and rum!

6. Continue tromping as in 1.

7. He is as tall as any tree.

7. As in 2.

8. Aloft, his head you hardly see.
a.   b.

8. At word "aloft," stretch out forefingers and point upward (a). At the word "head," bring fists together at about chin height to indicate a round head (b).

Hands form a visor above eyes at the word "see."

9. Rom and rum! - Rom and rum!
Rom and rum and rom and rum!

10. But his tremendous, G IA N T hat,

you can see that, you can see that!

11. Rom and rum! - Rom and rum!
Rom and rum and rom and rum!
Who tromps around through all the wood?
It is the GIANT Rommelgood!

12. Rom and rum! - Rom and rum!
Rom and rum and rom and rum!

9. Continue "tromping" as in 1.

10. Arms and hands outstretched to the sides show the rim of a huge hat. Stretch speech!
Continue showing the hat. At "can" smile and nod both times.

11. Repeat first verse as in 1 and 2.

12. Tromps again, slowing down.

It is recommended to continue with the following spatial movement game, "Rommelgood's Tromping Song." However, the hand gesture game can also stand by itself, as can the song.

Rommelgood's Tromping Song

ROMMELGOOD'S TROMPING SONG
Spatial movement singing game

Text

1. <u>Rom</u> and <u>rum</u> and <u>rom</u> and <u>rum</u>!

   <u>Rom</u> and <u>rum</u> and <u>rom</u> and <u>rum</u>!

2. I am the G I A N T Rommelgood!
   I tromp around through all the wood.
         v

3. Rom and rum and rom and rum!
   Rom and rum and rom and rum!

4. I am a G I A N T great big man
   with G I A N T steps I cross the land.
      v   v

5. Rom and rum and rom and rum!
   Rom and rum and rom and rum!

6. I am as tall as any tree.
   Aloft, my head you hardly see.

7. Rom and rum and rom and rum!
   Rom and rum and rom and rum!

8. But my tremendous, G I A N T hat,
                        v

   you can see that, you can see that!
        v   v

Gestures

1. At the accent in the melody line (____) make a long, elastic step. Make each step purposefully, slightly and elastically bending the knee.

   The steps are long and heavy, not loud. The giant tromps, he does not stomp.

   Move clockwise with right shoulder toward center of circle.

2. Stop. Stretch arms up high, with hands forming fists: Giant Rommelgood. On "around" nod, but leave arms stretched.

3. Again tromp clockwise around the circle as in 1.

4. Stop, then stretch arms and fists upward as in 2. Nod on "giant steps."

5. Again tromp clockwise around the circle as in 1.

6. As above in 2, make yourself tall.

7. Again tromp clockwise around the circle as in 1.

8. Show a wide hat with arms and hands outstretched to each side. Nod at "hat" and "that."

9. Rom and rum and rom and rum!
Rom and rum and rom and rum!
I am the G I A N T Rommelgood!
I tromp around through all the wood.

10. Then I go home, for home is best.
Rom and rum and rom and rum!
Rom and rum and rom and rum!

11. Now I sit and take a rest.

9. As in 1 and 2.

10. First tromp around in a circle clockwise as in 1, then return to your starting place from the beginning of the game. One can also keep going in a circle and stop wherever one finds oneself.

11. Now either sit on stools or the floor and at "take a rest" cover head with arms.
Alternatively, stop anywhere in the room, crouch down, elbows resting on knees, and head resting in hands. Stay quiet for a bit.

Conclusion
In order to calm the children down again after the lively tromping, the following song, "Quiet Diddledoo," can be sung, hummed, or played on the pentatonic Choroi flute.

Quiet Diddledoo

After the quiet song, while rising, the teacher can say: "Rommelgood has rested!"
If the "tromping step" still remains with the children, the following verse will be helpful:
> *Rommelgood tromps: rom and rum and rom and rum.*
> *With steps so soft and small, there go the children all:*
> *so — so — so — so — so — so — soo.*

Show everything in movement.

Song of Trolls and Gnomes

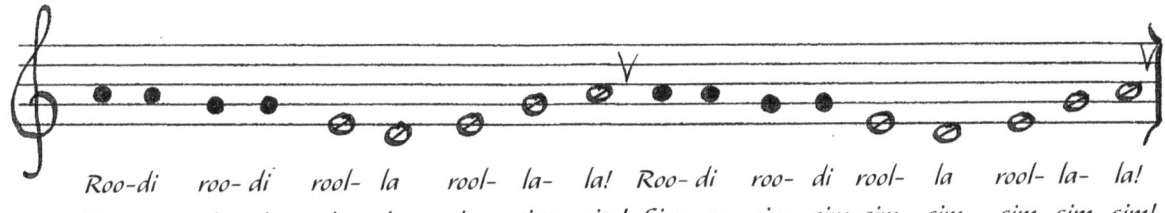

1. On a grassy knoll, grassy knoll,
danced a giant troll, giant troll.
Roodi roodi roolla, roollala!
Roodi roodi roolla, roollala!

2. On the mountain top, ... *
little gnomies hop, ...
Simse rim-sim sim sim, sim sim sim!
Simse rim-sim sim sim, sim sim sim!

3. The troll comes from his home, ...
he wants to catch a gnome, ...
Roodi roodi ...

4. Slip the gnomes, hop, hop, ...
into the mountain top, ...
Simse rim-sim ...

5. They slip into their homes, ...
He cannot find the gnomes, ...
Simse rim-sim ...

6. Tromps the giant troll, ...
homewards to his knoll, ...
Roodi roodi ...

7. Come the gnomes, hop, hop, ...
Back to the mountain top, ...
Simse rim-sim ...

8. The troll, he now goes home, ...
He could not catch a gnome, ...
Roodi roodi ...

9. Jolly on the Mountain-top, ...
The gnomes all dance and hop, ...
Simse rim-sim ...

The game can be developed further by inserting verses 8a to 11a (after verse 7):

8a. But look, the troll turns 'round, ...
grabs a gnomie, roundabout, ...
Roodi roodi ...

9a. This gnome goes with the troll, ...
back to his grassy knoll, ...
Roodi roodi ...

10a. But gnomie knows a trick, ...
runs away from the troll quick, ...
Simse rim-sim ...

11a. The gnomes all dance and hop, ...
Jolly on the mountain top, ...
Simse rim-sim ...

  * Always repeat the last three syllables of each line, as shown in the first stanza.

NOLL THE TROLL
Rhythmical-musical movement game with whole-body gestures

Noll the troll from Rumplehome,
would like to be small as a gnome!
Then quietly through the land he'd stroll.
But a famous crash-maker is that troll
when he tramps with his clumsy feet:

Rummel-pummel-rummel-hacks!
Rummel-pummel-rummel-cracks!
Rummel-pummel-rummel-smash!
Rummel-pummel-rummel-crash!

Too scared to stay, the rest run away.
Noll stands still and looks all around.
No one there - not a sound!
Slowly tramps the troll back home.
Tramp-tramp-tramp-tramp-tramp-tramp-tramp.

He sits down in his Rumplehome
and thinks - and thinks something up!
He takes two pieces of soft, soft moss,
of soft, soft, moss,
to stick on the sole of his shoe,
to stick on the sole of his shoe.
Now, when he takes a stroll,
so-so-so-soo,
so very quiet is that troll.
He takes a stroll from Rumplehome -
so-so-so-soo,
so-so-so-soo -
almost as quiet as a gnome:
so-so-so-soo,
so-so-so-soo,
Oh - yes!

Text
1. Noll, the troll

2. from Rumplehome,
   •   •

Gestures
1. Stand with legs wide and fists raised above head to each side. Note: "Noll" rhymes with "troll."

2. Keeping feet in wide stance, beat fists on each other at stomach height twice at • .

3. would sometimes like to be small as a gnome!

3. Now bring feet together on "like" and bend knees to appear smaller. Bow upper body lightly forward and create pointed hat with hands on forehead — approximately at hairline, not higher, because the young child can not yet bring hands together above head.

4. Then quietly through the land he'd stroll.
      r   l   r   l

4. Keeping the body posture described in 3, move around the room as quietly as possible with small, quiet steps.

5. But a famous crash-maker is that troll

5. Now rise up again to full size and raise fists as in 1 (see above). At "crash-maker" stamp strongly on the floor with the right foot.

6. when he tramps with his clumsy feet:
   l   r   l   r
Rummel-pummel-rummel-hacks!
  l   r   l   r
Rummel-pummel-rummel-cracks!
  l   r   l   r
Rummel-pummel-rummel-smash!
  l   r   l   r
Rummel-pummel-rummel-crash!
  l   r   l   r

6. Lower arms again and let them hang. Tramp with bent knees and big steps around the room. In addition, speak powerfully, particularly stressing the words "hacks," "cracks," "smash," and "crash."

7. Too scared to stay, the rest run away.

7. At "scared," clap hands flat against chest, stopping the movement. At "run away," spread your arms to the right and left with a flourish in front of you.

8. Noll stands still and looks all around.
No one there - not a sound!
     v   v

8. "Noll" stands speechless: place both hands to make a visor on forehead and turn around very slowly in place while speaking the text until "around." After this word, turn around silently in place at first, then speak the text so that you come back to the starting position on "there." Then bring hands back down silently and say, "not a sound," while nodding twice.

9. Slowly tramps the troll back home.
    r   l   r   l
Tramp-tramp-tramp-tramp-tramp-tramp-tramp –
    r   l   r   l   r   l   r   l

9. With head and arms hanging and knees bending, tramp around the room. You can repeat the text, or silently continue tramping a few steps further.

10. He sits down in his Rumplehome

10. Sit either on a stool or the floor.

11. and thinks - and thinks something up!

11. Assume the posture of someone who is busy thinking with head supported by hands. At "thinks something up," raise head. Voice becomes light as if to say, "I know something." Leave a lot of time for this last line.

12. He takes two pieces

12. At "takes," take some imaginary moss and hold hand wide open, showing the "moss."

13. of soft, soft moss,
    r on l hand
of soft, soft moss,
    l on r hand

13. With right hand press lightly on moss in left hand. Then switch hands, left on top of right hand.

14. to stick on the sole of his shoe,
    heel   middle   toes

to stick on the sole of his shoe.
    heel   middle   toes

14. With left hand, raise and hold your left lower leg tightly so that you can "glue" the moss with your right hand, pressing first on the heel of your left foot then the middle, and then the ball and toes. Repeat the same gesture, using the opposite foot and hand.

15. Now when he takes a stroll,
                  r   l

15. Stand up, and, swaying in place at "takes a stroll," step once with right foot and once with the left foot.

16. so-so-so-soo,
    r l r l

16. Now walk around the room cautiously, stepping with each foot so you barely hear anything.

17. so very quiet is that troll.
      r   l   r   l   v

17. Continue on as in 16, stopping for a moment after the word "troll." Stand and nod at v.

18. He takes a stroll from Rumplehome -
          •   •

19. so-so-so-soo,
so-so-so-soo -

20. almost as quiet as a gnome:

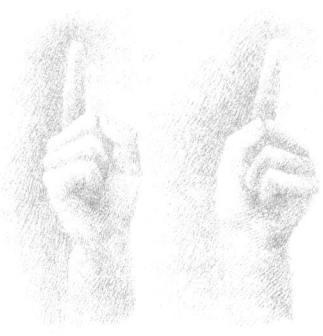

21. so-so-so-soo,
so-so-so-soo.

22. Oh - yes!

18. At "He," take the position as in 1 (see above). At "'Rumpelhome," pound the left hand twice at the • with the right hand.

19. Continue stepping as in 16.

20. Now stand still and raise both pointer fingers chest high, emphasizing "quiet" (see picture at left). At "gnome" put a pointed hat on head as in 3 above.

21. With pointed hat on and lightly stooping, move along with almost silent steps.

22. Stay standing, straightening up and letting arms hang on either side. At "Oh," raise head, and nod at "Yes" in affirmation.

NOLL THE TROLL IS RESTING!
Complementary gesture game to the movement game "Noll the Troll"

Noll the troll settles down,
resting tired limbs upon the ground.
He wants to rest a little while.

Heavily, he rests his head –
so with his hands, he makes a bed.

There comes a gentle breeze:
Hhhhhfff! - hhhhhfff!
Caresses him with gentle ease.
Hhhhhfff - hhhhhfff - hhhhfffff!
Then blows softly by: hhhhhfff!

Noll the troll stays alone,
sleeping quietly in his home.
Sleep - sleep - sleep---
Have a little re---st,
here comes the bree---ze:
Hhhhhfff! - hhhhhfff!
Caresses him in sleep with ease.
Hhhhhfff - hhhhhfff - hhhhfffff!
Then takes its leave:
Schsch - schschschsch!
Awake, Noll the troll, awake!
He stretches, stretches, well rested!
(Let's play again right away.)

Text
1. Noll the troll settles down,

Gestures
1. Stand with legs wide apart and fists raised overhead. On the word "settles" sit down on knees or on a stool. Note: "Noll" rhymes with "troll."

2. resting tired limbs upon the ground.
    r   l

2. Lift arms one after another at r and l and let them fall hard on thighs.

3. He wants to rest a little while.

3. Let head fall forward. One can see how hard it is to hold up your heavy head.

4. Heavily, he rests his head –
so with his hands, he makes a bed.

4. Support arms on thighs and hold head with your hands. Stay sitting like this for awhile.

5. There comes a gentle breeze:
Hhhhhfff! - hhhhhfff!

5. Now lift head and place hands on either side of mouth like a funnel. Through this funnel blow air "hhhhfff" without using your voice.

6. Caresses him with gentle ease.
Hhhhhfff - hhhhhfff - hhhhfffff!

7. Then blows softly by: hhhhhfff!

8. Noll the troll stays alone,

9. sleeping quietly in his home.

10. Sleep - sleep - sleep---
have a little re---st,

11. here comes the bree---ze:
Hhhhhfff!- hhhhhfff!

12. Caresses him in sleep with ease.
Hhhhhfff - hhhhhfff - hhhhfffff!

13. Then takes its leave:

　　→　　→
　→　→
Schsch - schschschsch!
→　　　→
→　→

14. Awake, Noll the troll, awake!

15. He stretches, stretches, well rested!

16. (Let's play again right away.)

---

6. Straighten up a little and with both hands, stroke torso twice. On the third time slowly stroke down from the head, over the torso, to the knees, taking your time.

7. As above in 5, but now during the blowing, let hands move forward towards the room with the breath.

8. While sitting, make the "troll gesture," which means to raise fists overhead. At "stays alone," bring arms down.

9. Support your heavy head once again in your arms.

10. With supported head, rock gently back and forth. At "rest," hold still and stay sitting a little while. The word "rest" is drawn out longer.

If you want to end the game without repeating anything, say the following: "He is quiet as a mouse, rests in his house and doesn't go out." Then slowly straighten up, shaking head, "no."

If you want to repeat the game, continue with 11.

11. See above as in 5. The word "breeze" is drawn out longer.

12. As in 6 above but slowly and gently with lowered eyelids.

13. Move hands in a forward direction at each arrow, palms facing forward towards children, letting the "sch sch sch sch" sound with intensity.

14. First stretch arms, then rub eyes. If sitting on knees, rise to kneeling, if sitting on floor, rise to standing in order to rub and stretch as in 15:

15. "He stretches" - right side, "he stretches" - left side, "rested" - both arms.

16. Stand up.

Another possibility for the rest time: From 1 to 8 remains the same, then continue with the following:

9a. And goes to sleep.

9a. Sit on knees (if sitting on a stool, move to floor) and bow upper body as low as you can, laying forearms next to legs on the floor. Lay head in hands on the floor.

10a. Sleep-sleep-sleep, re---st a little while.

10a. Stay quiet in this position. If some children lie on the floor, let them.

11a. Again, here comes the bree---ze:
Hhhhhfff!- hhhhhfff!

12a. Caresses him in sleep with ease.
Hhhhhfff - hhhhhfff - hhhhfffff!

11a and 12a. Rise up carefully, almost imperceptibly, and stroke the closest child. As quietly as possible, move from child to child and stroke gently over each child's head and back, all the while speaking the text repeatedly as needed to finish the gesture. If there are more than 8 children, stroke two at a time so the procedure doesn't take too long.

13a. Then takes its leave:
Schsch - schschschsch!

14a. Awake, Noll the troll, awake!

13a. Now call out intensely the "Sch" with gestures as in 13 (see above) and move to sitting on knees.

14a. From here, continue on with 14 to 16 as above.

If this game is played in a Parent and Child class, the parent stays beside the child and takes on the role of the caressing wind, stroking the child's head and back.

THE WATERMAN
Rhythmical-musical sound-word game with gestures

Droppela - dropella - dropella drop!
The rain came down both night and day.
Dropella - dropella - dropella - drop!
So much water has come our way.
Dropella - dropella - dropella - drop!
The water rises, the water swells.
Dropella - dropella - dropella - drop!
The lake is so full, it fills the wells.

He's full of glee, our Waterman,
for now he splashes on the land.
He climbs out of his water house:
splub - splob - splub - he's out!
Splish - splash - splish - splash -
splish - splash - splash!
Squish - squash - squish - squash -
squish - squash - squash!
So splashes now our Waterman.

Splash - splish, splish ...
Squash- squish, squish ...
Just listen how - he's splashing now!
Splash - splish - splish!
Squash -squish - squish!

Out comes the warm sun,
shining on the earth below.
All is dry once more.
The Waterman-
he flees the sun's warming rays.
Splish - splash, splash, splish,
splash, splash, splish!
And into the water -
splash! He jumps.
Gloog, gloog...gloog - gloog
Blub!
Blannnnnnnn!
He disappears, the Waterman.

Text
1. Droppela - dropella - dropella drop!

Gestures
1. Sitting, move hands, with lively finger movements, in parallel from up high down to thighs (table or floor). It is raining! Silently drum awhile.

2. The rain came down both night and day.

3. Dropella - dropella - dropella - drop!

4. So much water has come our way.

5. Dropella - dropella - dropella - drop!

6. The water rises, the water swells.

7. Dropella - dropella - dropella - drop!

8. The lake is so full,

9. it fills the wells.

10. He's full of glee, our Waterman,

2. Turn to the children, telling the story. Stretch out the word "night," and nod on "day."

3. Let it rain again as in 1. Continue the finger movement for a while after the text.

4. With both hands, palms facing down and outstretched fingers, indicate water level at knee height. Say the words "so much" stretched out.

5. As above in 1.

6. At, "rises," raise hands, still palm side down from knee high to several inches higher. For the "swelling", raise hands even higher, moving them apart and to the side in an arch.

7. As in 1 above.

8. Cross forearms at the wrists. From there move both hands, palm side down, in a flat arch moving away from each other and back, suggesting a broad expanse of water.

9. Round your arms as if you held a very large ball without your hands touching.

10. Raise hands up wide, palms facing the children, heavily and slowly.

11. for now he splashes on the land.

12. He climbs out of his water house:
             r   l   r   l

splub - splob - splub - he's out!
  r   l   r   l   r

13. Splish - splash - splish - splash -
        r   l   r   l

splish - splash - splash!
  r   l   r + l

14. squish - squash - squish - squash-
      ↑↑   ↓↓   ↑↑   ↓↓

squish - squash - squash!
  ↑↑   ↓↓   ↑↑

15. So splashes now our Waterman.
       r + l   r + l

Splash - splish, splish ...
 r + l   r + l   r + l

16. Squash- squish, squish ...

17. Just listen how - he's splashing now!

18. Splash - splish - splish!

19. Squash - squish - squish!

20. Out comes the warm sun,

11. At the word "now" slap thighs with both hands at the same time.

12. Bow forward until your hands touch the floor. Alternating right and left hand, indicate climbing out. Turn palms each time a little upward as if you want to scoop water out. Slowly straighten the upper body. The text and gestures should be coordinated with each other so that you arrive at the "water surface" by the end of the verse.

13. With flat hands, palms facing downward, splash vertically on alternate thighs. On the last "splash," slap both hands at the same time. If you are leading the game, sitting on the floor, then you can slap the floor.

14. Stroke thighs with both hands at the same time, forward and back (see arrows). When hands are forward by the knees, lift fingertips slightly up. When hands return to upper thigh, lift wrists up, suggesting waves. At the last "squash," lift hands up above knees.

15. At each r+l direction slap both hands flat on thighs.

16. As above in 14.

17. Cup both hands behind ears, listening. Then stretch speech, almost yelling, "l i s t e n."
At, "splashing," slap both hands again on the thighs and lift them high again.

18. As in 15 above.

19. As in 14 above.

20. Raise both hands overhead in a large round shape, with hands open to the children and fingers spread wide as sun rays, with thumbs touching each other. Let the sun shine for a while. If you are playing the game sitting on the floor, rise up to kneeling for the sun gesture.

21. shining on the earth below.

22. All is dry once more.

23. The Waterman -

24. he flees the sun's warming rays.

25. Splish - splash, splash, splish,
    r   l   r   l
splash, splish, splish!
  r   l   r + l

26. And into into the water -

27. splash! He jumps.

28. Gloog, gloog...gloog - gloog

29. [Silent movement]

21. The sun shines on, but now slowly slant "the sun" forward so it shines on the earth. Speak the accompanying text slowly.

22. Lay flat hands flat on knees, then close to body on thighs, feeling how dry the earth has become, moving gently and slowly.

23. Raise arms and hands high, with fingers spread.

24. Now wrap arms around head and duck a little. If you are playing the game on the floor, sit back on heels.

25. The Waterman hastens back to his pond; slap with a faster tempo on thighs, alternating right and left hands.

26. Raise hands high, palm side down, and "take off to jump in."

27. Bow forward and clap at "splash" in front of knees. At "he jumps," both hands in front of knees pointing toward the bottom of an imaginary pool, looking into it.

28. Cup right hand behind right ear and listen, then speak, "gloog -gloog." Then straighten up and look at the children. Bow forward, listening, and say again, "gloog - gloog."

29. Sit up straight letting hands hang down by your sides and look awhile at the imaginary pool.

30. Blub!

31. Blannnnnnnn!
◎ ◎

32. He disappears,

33. the Waterman.

30. Now show, with both hands in front of knees, a large bubble: the palms are facing the floor, the fingers are loosely curled inward, the pointer fingers are touching slightly at the knuckles. The fingers quickly open without changing the hands — the bubble popped!

31. Now draw with both index fingers, in mirror image, ripples in the imaginary pool. Then look at the "water."

32. Lay palms on top of each other and bow forward, continuing to look into the water, finger tips pointed down in front of knees as if getting ready to dive.

33. Lay hands slowly back on knees, straighten up, and speak with a confirming nod, "the Waterman."

MERMAID IN THE MOONLIGHT
Rhythmical-musical story with gestures

*In the shining moonlight's glow,
the mermaid sits upon a stone.
And as she combs her long, long hair,
she looks into the water below.*

*Bending further, in full detail
there she sees her silvery tail!
Silvery tail! Silvery tail!
She has no feet - on which to stand.
She has no feet - to walk the land.
She has no feet - to dance around,
to dance around, without fail.
For she has got a silvery tail,
a silvery tail!*

*In the shining moonlight's glow,
the mermaid sits upon a stone.
Gently splishing, gently splashing,
listen to the water ring,
hear the little mermaid sing:*

She speaks:
"In water fresh, in water fresh,
I play with snails, I play with fish.
Hear the raindrops ring:
pling - pling - pling - pling - pling - pling - pling -
pling - pling - pling -
pling - pling - pling -
when on the water they do spring:
plingngng - plingngng - plingngng!

I can swim - swim - swim.
Let me swing upon the tide."

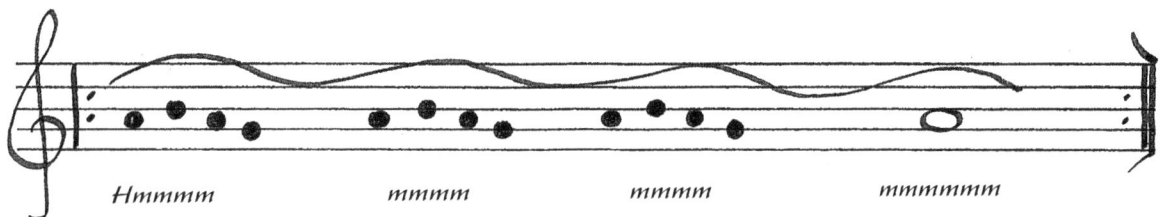

Hmmmm   mmmm   mmmm   mmmmmm

In the shining moonlight's glow,
the mermaid sits upon a stone.
The moon from heaven high goes down;
the mermaid also slides right down,
Slips into the water below.
Once more she stretches up to peek,
then slips again into water's gleam
and rolls inside her silvery tail
to sleep and dream, to dream
of dancing, dancing without fail.

Text	**Gestures**
1. In the shining moonlight's glow, 	1. It is a "full moon" so make a bowl shape with rounded palms and pinky edges together as if there is a ball inside. Slowly lead hands upward with fingertips pointing up. Speak, stretching the syllable "light," and let the moon shine a little while longer.
2. the mermaid sits upon a stone.	2. Bring hands down to press palms lightly on thighs.
3. And as she combs her l<u>o</u>ng, l<u>o</u>ng h<u>ai</u>r,	3. With both palms, "comb" the imaginary long hair on each side from crown to thighs, without moving the rest of the body. Make this "combing" gesture at each underlined vowel.
4. she looks into the water below. 	4. Lay hands like a visor over forehead and bow forward just a little with upper body to look into the "water."
5. Bending further, in full detail	5. Now bow deeply forward until upper body rests on thighs.

6. there she sees her silvery tail!

6. With the upper body still resting on thighs, bring outstretched fingers together, with fingers closed, only fingertips touching and thumbs crossed as "tail fin" (see picture at left). Bring hands, held in this position, down in front of legs until fingertips point between the toes. Stretch the word "there" in speech.

7. Silvery tail!
Silvery tail!   [silent movement]

7. At "tail," bring hands slightly forward and move them diagonally upwards while straightening upper body again. Only when the "tail fin" reaches knee height, and as you say "silvery tail" again, wag the tail first left, then right, as shown by arrows. Repeat wagging left and right once more silently.

8. She has no feet -

8. Dissolve tail gesture and place palms firmly on thighs with fingers together indicating two "feet." At the word "no," shake head.

9. on which to stand.

9. Now press the "feet" lightly on thighs.

10. She has no feet -

10. As above in 8.

11. to walk the land.
      r   l

11. Now take a step with each "foot," first right, then left.

12. She has no feet -

12. As above in 8.

13. to dance around,

13. Hold the "feet" again on thighs, circle them clockwise at the same time, staying close to the thighs, three times total, as indicated under the text.

to dance around, without fail.

91

14. For she has got a silvery tail,

⌣

   a silvery tail!

⌣

15. In the shining moonlight's glow, the mermaid sits upon a stone.

16. Gently splishing, gently splashing,

17. listen to the water ring,

18. hear the little mermaid sing:

19. [music below]

14. Bring hands back together as "tail fin" and wag in front of knees as described above in 7, this time more slowly as indicated under text.

15. As above in 1.

16. "Splash" with both hands around knees in the "water."

17. Bring both hands to cup ears and listen.

18. Lay both hands together in lap.

19. Sway upper body lightly back and forth to the swing of the melody. Sing with a tender voice.

La la-lay- la, la la-loo- la, la- lay- la, soft and bright.
La la-lay- la, la la-loo- sings the mer- maid with de- light.

Lay- la- la- loo- lay- la- la- loo

20. She speaks:

21. "In water fresh, in water fresh

⌣⌣ ⌣⌣ ⌣⌣ ⌣⌣

22. I play with snails,

20. Look at the children kindly.

21. Play with both hands in the imaginary water in front of and below knees. The hands follow the speech rhythm, moving to and from each other as shown by arrows at left.

22. Keeping right fist close to hip on the right thigh, stretch pointer and pinky fingers forward as "feelers." Slowly the "snail" creeps towards the knee.

23. I play with fish.

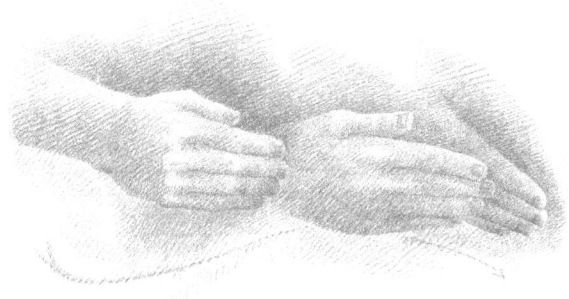

23. Hold right hand in front of and below the knee in the "water," with fingers stretched and held together, little finger parallel to floor, and thumb lying on top, as "the fish." Make smooth swimming movements led by the fingertips from right to left in front of knees.

24. Hear the raindrops ring:

24. For the word "hear," bring right hand to right ear. Afterward, bring both hands silently a little over head and at "raindrops," let it rain down with lightly wiggling fingers. At the word "ring," tap thighs with fingertips and thumbs.

25. pling - pling - pling - pling -
    r   l   r   l
pling - pling - pling -
  r   l   r
pling - pling - pling -
  l   r   l
Pling - pling - pling -
  r   l   r

25. With index fingertips, tap thighs, alternating right and left. Another possibility: flick softly with thumb and pointer of each hand (as if to flick a ladybug off your thigh), alternating right and left on thighs.

26. when on the water they do spring:
plingngng - plingngng - plingngng!

26. At the word "spring" and each time at "pling-" tap (or flick softly) with both hands at the same time.

27. I can swim - swim - swim.

27. Bring hands together as "tail fin" (see picture at left) and wiggle it toward children as shown by the arrows.

28. Let me swing upon the tide.

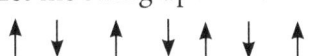

28. After "swimming" bring the "tail fin" back closer to body and move it back and forth according to speech rhythm as shown by arrows.

29. [Quiet humming]

29. While quietly humming the melody, let the "tail fin" continue to swing back and forth carefully and quietly.

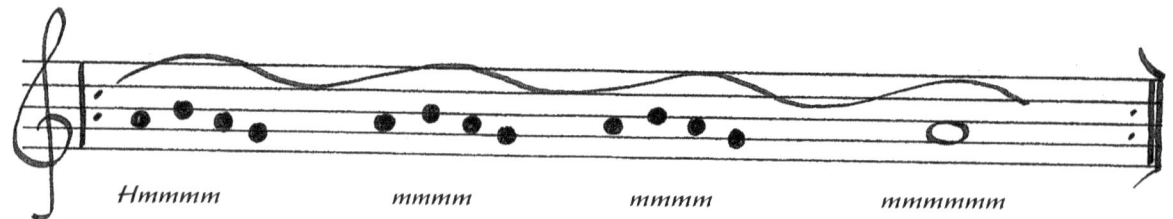

Hmmmm   mmmmm   mmmmm   mmmmmmm

30. In the shining moonlight's glow,
the mermaid sits upon a stone.

30. As above in 1.

31. The moon from heaven high goes down;

31. Continue to show the moon high in the sky. After the words "heaven high," pause a little, and at "goes down," let the moon set softly on thighs.

32. the mermaid also slides right down,

32. Form the "tail fin" gesture close to the stomach and then direct it forward along thighs toward knees, until the fingertips hang over knees at the word "down."

33. slips into the water below.

33. At the word "slips" the "tail fin" dives with momentum into the water. Then, dissolving the "tail fin" gesture, straighten up and let arms rest by your sides, with your gaze still on the water.

34. Once more she stretches up to peek.

34. Form a fist with right hand in front of knees, stretch out index finger with back of hand facing self. Bring the fist slowly up to chest height, straightening upper body as you go. At the word "peek" make a deliberate movement with index finger toward the children.

35. then slips again into water's gleam

35. Now the index finger leads the movement: it plunges down until it reaches shin height.

36. and rolls inside her silvery tail

36. Hands again form the "tail fin," this time to the right of the right knee. From there, the "tail" makes a big arc in front until it reaches the left shoulder. At "silvery tail", lay the outside of left hand on the left shoulder and lay the cheek on the outside of right hand in a resting gesture.

37. to sleep and dream, to dream

37. Slowly lower the right arm and tilt the head even lower to the left, closing the arms.

38. of dancing, dancing without fail.
⌣ ⌣ ⌣ ⌣

38. Stay in the sleep gesture awhile and rock side to side with the speech rhythm, in the direction of the arrows.

THE MERMAID'S DREAM
Dance with gestures

Note: The song tells a story, so the tempo is adjusted to the movement of the narrative. The pauses between the various movement sequences can also be longer or shorter. Holding firmly to the measure or note values is not required. That is why the beats are only indicated, because the whole song should be sung fluently, adapted to the story: sleeping and dreaming under the willow tree is to be sung more slowly, stretching out the notes. The disappearance of the scaly tail and the dancing are then sung more with a more lively, rhythmic pulsation.

Text

1. The mermaid slumbers in the lake.

2. A lovely dream has she.

3. She walks around as if awake

4. under the willow tree, under the willow tree.

5. [silent movement]

Gestures

1. All crouch down, resting left cheek on joined hands as if sleeping.

2. Smile while lightly rocking.

3. Gradually rise to standing.

4. Lift arms high to the side with hands hanging down loosely like hanging branches. Don't stretch arms

5. Lower arms and join hands, fingertips pointing forward with thumbs crossing (tail tip).

6. The fish's tail has gone away.

7. The mermaid walks so light and free.
With tender feet she may now dance
the round-a-lay.

Round-a-round-a-round-a-lay,
round-a-round-a-lay.

8. Under the willow tree, under the willow tree,

9. in dream,

10. in dream, in dream.

6. Separate hands, showing that the tail is not there any more.

7. Make a quarter turn to the left, so that right shoulder points to center of circle. Walk around the room clockwise. The path does not have to be exactly on the circle line.

Repeat as needed. During the last time slow down the tempo in transition to the willow tree gesture.

8. As above in 4.

9. Slowly crouch down.

10. Lay head with left cheek on closed palms in sleeping gesture and close eyes.
Remain seated for a bit.

THE PLAYFUL HOBGOBLIN
Rhythmic-musical hand gesture game

*Do you know the playful hobgoblin,
the one that rollicks and romps?
She dances at night —
Watch! What a sight!*

*Rumple de pumple - rumple de pumple!
Waddle de waddle - waddle de waddle!
Bumble de mumble - bumble de mumble!
Figgle de foggle - figgle de foggle!
Tompedee doze, stands on her toes!
So so de sow -
runs forward a bit.
So so de sow -
runs back a bit.
Tompedee doze, stands on her toes!*

*Stamps with her feet:
Trampledee tramp, trampledee tramp.
Claps with her hands:
clapperdee clap, clapperdee clapp.
Trampledee tramp, trampledee tramp.
Clapperdee clap, clapperdee clapp.*

*Stops at a click
to show us her trick:
she stands alone, one foot on the ground,
proudly looks all around —
and does not fall down!*

*Now the little one
begins once more the dancing fun:
Rumple de pumple - rumple de pumple!
Waddle de waddle - waddle de waddle!
Bumble de mumble - bumble de mumble!
Figgle de foggle - figgle de foggle!
Tompedee doze, stands on her toes!*

*Oh!
What has she heard?
Hey?
Something has disturbed!*

*Tripple de tripple.
Scampers into the hole in the ground!
Look closely, she might still be found.*

*Whoops!
The goblin's away, did not want to stay!*

*Now, dear one,
The game is done.*

Text

1. Do you know the playful hobgoblin,

2. the one that rollicks and romps?

3. She dances at night —

4. Watch! What a sight!

5. Rumple de pumple - rumple de pumple!

6. Waddle de waddle - waddle de waddle!

7. Bumble de mumble - bumble de mumble!

8. Figgle de foggle - figgle de foggle!

9. Tompedee doze, stands on her toes!

10. So so de sow -

11. runs forward a bit.

12. So so de sow -

Gestures

1. Look around questioningly.

2. On "one" nod with vigor. On "rollicks" lift balled fists and on "romps" quickly turn fists around each other.

3. With pointers sticking out move hands to and fro.

4. At "watch" lift fists and at X move them quickly forward and back.

5. Right fist beats on left, lower fist in speech rhythm, four times, each time swinging upward a little so that the movement is not abrupt.

6. While holding fists to right and left at sides of head (at ear height) shift body center to right and left in speech rhythm, not too pronounced and not too quick.

7. Duck down, putting both hands in front of your mouth like a megaphone. In this position bounce a bit up and down, while mumbling mysteriously.

8. Sit upright again with arms up high. Turn hands in and out, with relaxed wrists and fingers. There is no accent on the turning, only a lively whirling (a little above head).

9. Stretch upward holding fists high with pointers stretched out.

10. Note: "sow" rhymes with "now." Turn fists around each other, starting near the stomach, first slowly...

11. ...then accelerating while moving forward (away from your body).

12. As in 10, but turn fists in opposite direction.

13. runs back a bit.

14. Tompedee doze, stands on her toes!

15. St<u>a</u>mps with her f<u>ee</u>t:

tr<u>a</u>mpledee tr<u>a</u>mp, tr<u>a</u>mpledee tr<u>a</u>mp.

16. Claps with her hands:
    x   x
clapperdee clap, Clapperdee clapp.
 x   x x   x

17. Trampledee tramp, trampledee tramp.

18. Clapperdee clap, Clapperdee clapp.

19. Stops at a click

20. to show us her trick:
  ↑   ↑

21. she stands alone, one foot on the ground,

22. proudly looks all around —
   ⌒   ⌒

23. and does not fall down!

24. N<u>ow</u> the l<u>itt</u>le <u>one</u>
beg<u>ins</u> once m<u>ore</u> the d<u>a</u>ncing f<u>un</u>:

25. Rumple de pumple - rumple de pumple!
Waddle de waddle - waddle de waddle!
Bumble de mumble - bumble de mumble!
Figgle de foggle - figgle de foggle!
Tompedee doze, stands on her toes!

26. Oh!
What has she heard?

27. Hey?
Something has disturbed!

13. As in 11, but move fists back towards body.

14. Stretch arms up as high as possible with pointers straight up. Stretch the whole upper body.

15. With flat hands, slap thighs lightly (right and left in turn) in speech rhythm.

16. Clap lightly with a bounce. Hands make a small circle, moving in and out. Emphasize the "p" on "clapp."

17. As in 15.

18. As in 16.

19. Hold hands quiet, palms facing, at throat height.

20. Lower left hand. Lift up right pointer and move it twice toward the children.

21. Lift right fist above head with thumb stretched out. The other fingers are rolled together.

22. Turn fist with outstretched thumb to left, then right.

23. Wiggle thumb to and fro (negation).

24. At chest height bounce both fists up and down, upper body bounces along.

25. As in 5 to 9.

26. Drop hands suddenly, hold right hand to ear.

27. Bend forward, hands propped up on knees, and look questioningly to right and left, hesitating a little, as if waiting.

28. Tripple de tripple.

29. Scampers into the hole in the ground!

30. Look closely, she might still be found.

31. Whoops!
The goblin's away, did not want to stay!

32. Now, dear one,
the game is done.

28. On thighs, tiptoe along knees toward body with pointer tips (making little steps).

29. Left fist on thigh, fingers down. Right pointer slips into hollow fist.

30. Pointer peeps out at end of fist, wiggling a little.

31. Pointer tip disappears in fist. Looking at empty fist, say "The goblin's away." Nod and call: "did not want to stay!"

32. Open arms and hands, showing them empty.

If the goblin dance follows, omit 32.

THE HOBGOBLIN DANCE
Movement game with gestures

The playful Hobgoblin dances in the night.
Watch! What a sight!
Rumple de pumple - rumple de pumple!
Waddle de waddle - waddle de waddle!
Bumble de mumble - bumble de mumble!
Figgle de foggle - figgle de foggle!
Tompedee doze, stands on her toes!
So so de sow -
runs forward a bit.
So so de sow -
runs back a bit.
Tompedee doze, stands on her toes!
Stands on her toes! Tompedee doze.
Stamps with her feet:
Trampledee tramp, trampledee tramp.
Claps with her hands:
clapperdee clap, clapperdee clapp.
Trampledee tramp, trampledee tramp.
Clapperdee clap, clapperdee clapp.
Yes!
Trampledee trampledee trampledee trampledee
trampledee trampledee trampledee tramp.

The Hobgoblin dances in a round,
trampledee trample on Goblin ground.
Trampledee trampledee trampledee tramp!
She stops! Quick!
To show us a trick:
stands alone, one foot on the ground
proudly looks all around —
and does not fall down!

Now the little one
begins once more the dancing fun:
Rumple de pumple - rumple de pumple!
Waddle de waddle - waddle de waddle!
Bumble de mumble - bumble de mumble!
Figgle de foggle - figgle de foggle!
Tompedee doze, stands on her toes!
Oh!
What has she heard?

Hey?
Something has disturbed!
Tripple de tripple.
Scampers into the hole in the ground!
Look closely, she might still be found.
The Hobgoblin's inside, she sits and hides.
Now, dear one - our game is now done!
We are done - we are done!
Now a little treat - Just one!

Our Hobgoblin wishes to greet
and gives each child a little treat
Mouth open so wide,
here it comes—right inside...
Yummmm! It tastes so fine.
Thank you for this treat of mine.

Text

1. The playful Hobgoblin dances in the night.

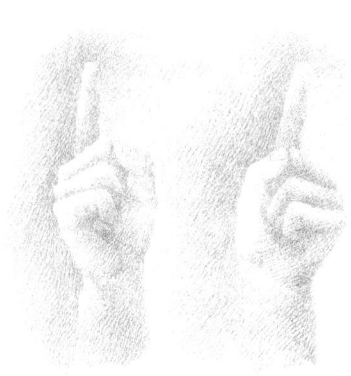

Gestures

1. After the preceding seated game is finished, stand up and at "playful" stretch hands up straight with forefingers pointed upwards. The gesture is accentuated. Then in this position, swing both hands back and forth.

2. Watch! What a sight!

2. Make closed fists again, this time at stomach height. At "watch" move fists above and over in a very small arch toward the children and at "what" them back to the beginning position.

3. Rumple de pumple - rumple de pumple!
   x   x   x   x

3. At each X lightly bounce left fist off of right fist, springing back each time so that the movement isn't too abrupt.

4. Waddle de waddle - waddle de waddle!

4. Hold fists to right and left at sides of head (at ear level) and shift body weight according to direction shown by arrows under the text at left. Not too strong and not too fast.

5. Bumble de mumble - bumble de mumble!

5. Crouch forward and hold hands like a megaphone in front of mouth. In this position, spring up and down a little on knees. Say, "Bumble de mumble" mysteriously.

6. Figgle de foggle - figgle de foggle!

6. Standing back up, stretch arms high and, with loose wrists and fingers, turn hands in and out. There is no accent on the turning, only a lively whirling (a little above head).

7. Tompedee doze, stands on her toes!

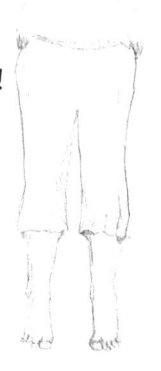

7. Rise up on tiptoes, stretch hands up vertically and point to the sky with both index fingers (as in picture at left). Stay a while in this position, then lower both arms back down.

8. So so de sow -

9. runs forward a bit.

10. So so de sow -

11. runs back a bit.

12. Tompedee doze, stands on her toes! Stands on her toes! Tompedee doze.

13. St<u>a</u>mps with her f<u>ee</u>t:

tr<u>a</u>mpledee tr<u>a</u>mp, tr<u>a</u>mpledee tr<u>a</u>mp.

14. Claps with her hands:
    X   X

clapperdee clap, clapperdee clapp.
X   X   X   X

15. Trampledee tramp, trampledee tramp.

16. Clapperdee clap, clapperdee clapp.

8. While standing in place, roll fists around each other, near your stomach, towards the children, slowly at first.

9. Then take 2 or 3 quiet steps forward into the circle, turning fists faster around each other.

10. Standing still again, turn fists around each other in the opposite direction (towards self), slowly at first.

11. Take 2 or 3 quiet steps backward, out from the center of the circle, turning fists even faster.

To simplify the movement, make a half turn to face outward from the middle of the circle and step forward at "runs back a bit."

12. Rise up on tiptoes stretching arms up vertically and point to the sky with both index fingers. You are from head down to feet an "i." In this position, turn around clockwise in place on balls of feet until you face the middle of the circle again, all the while saying, "stands on her toes" as often as needed until you reach your place. Conclude by speaking "Tompedee doze" while stretching fully.

13. Stamp strongly on the floor, alternating feet, at each underlined vowel. Speak powerfully with the movement. If the children can not follow the rhythm exactly, allow them to do it as they please. After frequent repetition, most children will be able to learn the rhythm.

14. Clap quietly and lightly, circling for each clap. Now speak tenderly. Do not correct the children if they can not yet follow the rhythm. Emphasize the "p" on "clapp."

15. See above as in 13.

16. See above as in 14.

17. Yes!
Trampledee trampledee trampledee trampledee trampledee trampledee trampledee tramp.
The Hobgoblin dances in a round,
trampledee trample on Goblin ground
Trampledee trampledee trampledee tramp!

17. Lift hands up and call out, stretching the word "Yes!" Meanwhile, turn so right shoulder points toward the middle of the circle and tromp around the circle clockwise with small steps to the rhythm of speech. Arrange the coordination of speech and movement so that you return to your standing point at the end of the verse.

18. She stops! Quick!

18. Lift hands with index fingers lightly outstretched, and call out, stretching the word "she." This is the preparation for standing still. At "stops," clap hands close to chest, thumbs against body. Now you are standing still and waiting until all the children are standing.

19. To show us a trick:

19. Let tight-held hands go and face palms forwards at shoulder height. When needed, turn yourself slowly to face the center.

20. stands alone, one foot on the ground

20. Now raise the left foot, not too high, and balance with arms out-stretched.

21. proudly looks all around—

21. Move your head very little, but look right and left, angling eyes mischievously.

22. and does not fall down!

22. Now shake head and place left foot back on the ground with arms remaining out wide to the sides.

23. [silent gesture]

24. Now the little one
begins once more the dancing fun:

25. Rumple de pumple - rumple de pumple!
Waddle de waddle - waddle de waddle!
Bumble de mumble - bumble de mumble!
Figgle de foggle - figgle de foggle!
Tompedee doze, stands on her toes!

26. Oh!

27. What has she heard?

28. [Silent gesture]

29. Hey?

30. Something has disturbed!

31. Tripple de tripple.

32. Scampers into the hole in the ground!

33. Look closely, she might still be found.

23. The Hobgoblin stands proudly on both legs as if to say, "I did that well," and keeps holding arms out wide to the side.

24. While you speak the text, bring arms slowly to chest height and make fists, getting ready to pound them on each other.

25. See above as in 3 through 7.

26. Bring our hands down, all of a sudden, and press fists against chest as if surprised, thereby standing also firmly on the floor with both feet.

27. Now cup right hand at right ear and bow slightly forward to listen.

28. The curious Hobgoblin moves very quietly on tiptoes, taking about four small steps, toward the center of the circle.

29. Stand still with upper body bowing forward and call, questioning, "Hey?" as if to say, "is anyone there?"

30. Still standing in the forward bow position, the Hobgoblin looks around searchingly to the right and to the left. She listens once more, then turns herself around and…

31. …hastens swiftly away, with very small steps, with back to the middle of the circle. Speak "Tripple de tripple" as long as it takes the Hobgoblin to get back to her "home."

32. Hide yourself somewhere in the room: under the table, behind the curtain or cabinet, in a corner, etc. The children look for the hidden one.

33. Call out briefly from your hiding place….

34. The Hobgoblin's inside, she sits and hides.

34. ...And retreat quickly back into hiding. Remain there for a moment and then come out and let the children hide as "the Hobgoblin" and search for them. They love that! Whoever is found can help you continue the search for those still hidden.

To avoid the game getting out of hand, one can arrange it so that the child who finds a Hobgoblin hiding can silently beckon to the teacher, who can look and say, "Yes, there is a Hobgoblin hiding." When everyone is found, then:

35. Now, dear one—our game is now done!

35. When possible, after this lively and dynamic game, children should receive something to nibble on to soothe them.

36. We are done—we are done!
Now a little treat—just one!
Our Hobgoblin wishes to greet
and gives each child a little treat.
Mouth open so wide,
here it comes—right inside…
Yummmm! It tastes so fine.
Thank you for this treat of mine.

36. You can share the following with the children: nuts, raisins, dried plums, or apple slices.

WILL O' THE WISPS
Rhythmic-musical story with gestures

It flimmers - it flimmers.
It shimmers - it shimmers.
It flits - it flits.
It glits - it glits.
It blits - zits - zits - zits.
What creatures? Tisp - tisps -
the Will-of-the-Wisps!
They tripple - they trapple.
They skip - pel - lel - lapple.
Now whirling - now twirling,
first here - then yon,
and wheeeee --
they're gone!

Text
1. It flimmers - it flimmers.

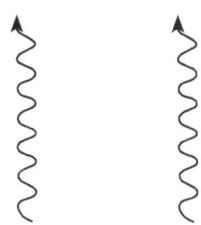

2. It shimmers - it shimmers.

3. It flits - it flits.

4. It glits - it glits.

Gestures
1. Holding hands next to each other, move them from below to above, twice. At the same time, lightly and quickly turn wrists in and out, making a restless movement like lapping flames.

2. Hold both hands, palms forward, at nose level; the hands are on either side of, and a little forward of, the face. Lightly move all fingers, like glowing coals.

3. Quickly move both arms diagonally forward, with pointer fingers extended, once to the left, once to the right.

4. Hold both fists (with rolled-in fingers forward) next to each other at chest height. At "glits" pointers dart out and are pushed up toward eye level. Then roll up pointers lightly and at the second "glits" let them dart out again above head.

5. It blits - zits - zits - zits.

5) Draw "lightning" into the air with the tips of both pointers, starting high left and moving down, right, left, right, down to thighs, in the shape of a thunderbolt. Speech and movement rhythmically exact!

6. What creatures? Tisp - tisps -

6. Hold fists (rolled-up fingers forward) with protruding pointers quietly next to each other at chest height. Tip left pointer forward at "Tisp" and right pointer forward at "Tisps".

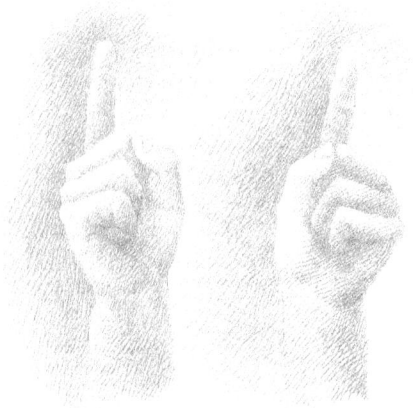

7. the Will-of-the-Wisps!
↑↑   ↑↑

7. "Throw" both index fingers up into the air, twice!

8. They tripple - they trapple.

8. Quickly open both fists and wave both hands (palms down) lightly side to side at waist height.

9. They skip-pel-lel-lapple.

9. Wave both hands (palms facing) lightly side to side, a little higher.

10. Now whirling - now twirling,

10. Arms circle outward on the high diagonal on each side of the body - like two cones.

11. first here - then yon

11. Point to the high diagonal with both hands, once to the left and once to the right.

12. and wheee—they're gone!

12. At "wheee," throw up hands and shake them for the long "eee," then hide them behind your back.

THE LITTLE GHOSTS o' NIGHT
Hand gesture game

Dong-dong-dong-dong-dong-dong-dong-dong-
 dong-dong-dong-dong!
Midnight!
Through the window panes
the full moon laughs down bright.
She woke them all right up,
the little ghosts o' night,
the little ghosts o' night.

They swia-swia-sway
to the ghosties' roundalay:
swia-swia-sway,
swia-swia-sway.

Each wobbles his little head about,
the ghost o' night, the little lout.
Wi-wa-wobble, ni-na-nobble,
wi-wa-wobble, ni-na-nobble.

And swia-swia-sway
to the ghosties' roundalay:
swia-swia-sway,
swia-swia-sway.

They turn a-noola-noola-nile
around, around a little while:
Noola-noola-noola-nile,
noola-noola-noola-nile.

And swia-swia-sway
to the ghosties' roundalay:
swia-swia-sway,
swia-swia-sway.

The fingers of the ghosts,
they tap on walls and posts.
Tasple-tasple, scrapple-scrapple,
tasple-tasple, scrapple-scrapple,
they scrapple: tasple-tasple-touse,
mysteriously all through the house.

And swia-swia-sway
to the ghosties' roundalay:
swia-swia-sway,
swia-swia-sway.

The good moon calls: So long, so long,
you ghosts o' night, I must be gone!
They wave to her: So long, dear moon!
So - - so - - so long!

Donnnng!
From the clock tower, it struck: One!

Hoo! Flisha-flisha-floosha-floosha,
 flisha-flisha-floosha-floosha.
Flisha-flisha-floosha-floosha,
 flisha-flisha-floosha-floosha.
Hee! To and fro: Hoosha-hoosha,
 hoosha-hoosha.
Hoo! Flisha-flisha-floosha-floosha,
 flisha-flisha-floosha-floosha.
Hee! To and fro: hoosha-hoosha,
 hoosha-hoosha.
 Hoosha-hoosha-hoosha-hoosha.
Hoo! hoosh --- hoosh!
Pssssst!
The little ghosts o' night are gone.
All are hidden, every one!

Text	**Gestures**
1. Dong-dong-dong-dong-dong-dong-dong-dong-dong-dong-dong-dong!	1. Suggest the striking of a bell by making a "clapper" with extended arms, the left hand cupped over the right fist, swinging back and forth; imagine the "clapper" striking the bell on each side. Let the "ng" ring out. It is a big church tower.
2. M i d n i g h t !	2. After the twelfth stroke, slowly bring hands to each side of mouth as a megaphone, and call, "Midnight!"
3. Through the window panes	3. Arms and hands form a window through which the moon laughs.
4. the full moon laughs down bright.	4. Looking out the window, rest hands on sides of the head, framing it, and laugh. Continue laughing silently a while.
5. She woke them all right up,	5. Rub eyes with fingers, very gently.
6. the little ghosts o' night the little ghosts o' night	6. Hold hands at eye level at sides of head, palms facing children, wiggling fingers in a lively way. Stoop a bit and pull back your head.
7. They swia - swia - sway to the ghosties' roundalay: swia - swia - sway - swia - swia -sway.	7. With parallel hands moving together, palms down, at waist height, make a gently waving gesture up and down towards the right and towards the left, alternating lines, twice. Speak very melodically, almost singing.
8. Each wobbles his little head about, the ghost o' night, the little lout. Wi-wa-wobble, ni-na-nobble Wi-wa-wobble, ni-na-nobble	8. Come to stillness. The transition is fluid. Wait until all have stopped. Then wobble your head from side to side, following the arrow directions. Continue wobbling for the next three lines, speaking rhythmically.
9. And swia - swia - sway to the ghosties' roundalay: swia - swia - sway - swia - swia -sway.	9. As above in 7.

10. They turn a-noola-noola-nile

Around, around a little while

Noola-noola-noola-nile

noola-noola-noola-nile

11. And swia - swia - sway
to the ghosties' roundalay:
swia - swia - sway -
swia - swia -sway.

12. The fingers of the ghosts,

13. They tap on walls and posts

14. Tasple - tasple, scrapple - scrapple

Tasple - tasple, scrapple - scrapple

15. They scrapple:
tasple - tasple - touse,

10. Bring hands forward, bending at the elbow, so the hands are at waist height. Hands hang down loosely. Make two horizontal circles with the hands, starting inside forward and circling around back horizontally as if stirring a bowl, two circles for each line.

11. As above in 7.

12. Hold hands up vertically, palms toward each other. In rhythm, lightly tap finger pads together two times.

13. For "walls": lift hands, palms forward, as if pressing against a "wall," twice. For "posts": flex hands back so palms are up and move hands up (above head height) as if pressing flat against a ceiling beam, twice.

14. Tap with all finger pads against "posts" above, once on each "Tasple." Scratch lightly on the vertical "walls" with all five fingers of each hand on each "scrapple," accent on s: sssssscrapple.

15. Continue as above, scratching with bent fingers on "scrapple" and tapping with outstretched fingers on "tasple."

16. Mysteriously all through

16. Keeping hands parallel and arms bent, move hands very slowly down an imaginary wall until hands and fingers touch the thighs, speaking mysteriously in a whisper on "Mysteriously all," syllables stretched: *Mysss-terioussss-ly all.*

Keeping hands parallel, move hands slowly upward, palms up and fingers quiet, drawing out the vowel sound as you whisper on "through": *throoouuugh.*

Caution: It is important to note that the "mysterious" situation must be formed objectively through the sound of the voice, articulation, and movement, out of the music of sound and word and out of speech rhythm. Avoid subjective emotion, mimicry and drama so as not to frighten the children when bringing this "mysterious" mood.

17. the house.

17. On "house" indicate a roof with your two hands overhead in a triangle with middle fingers touching: *the houssse.*

18. And swia - swia - sway
to the ghosties' roundalay:
swia - swia - sway -
swia - swia -sway.

18. As in 7, use melodious song-like speech.

19. The good moon calls: "So long. so long, you ghosts o' night, I must be gone!"

19. Make the gesture of the "Moon" (as above in 3). At "call" hold hands as a megaphone at mouth. Speak "So long, you ghosts of night, I must be gone," melodically.

20. They wave to her: So long dear moon,
So--so--so long!

20. Wave lightly and loosely with both hands.

21. Donnnnng!

22. From the clock tower:

23. It struck: One!

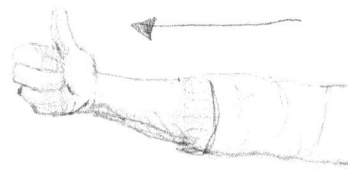

24. Hoo!

25. Flisha-flisha-floosha-floosha
flisha-flisha-floosha-floosha,

Flisha-flisha-floosha-floosha
flisha-flisha-floosha-floosha,

26. Hee!

27. To and fro:

28. Hoosha-hoosha- hoosha-hoosha
Hoosha-hoosha - hoosha-hoosha

29. Hooo!...

30. Hoosh---hoosh!

21. Gesture as in 1, clapper against bell, allowing the "nnnng" to sound for a long time while slowly raising fist.

22. Extend arms, hands held above the head, to form a clock tower.

23. Dissolve the tower gesture. On "One!" show right fist with thumb out.

24. Pull back head slightly and lay rolled-up fists on right and left cheeks. Let out a soft, breathy "Hooo!"

25. On "flisha-flisha…" thrust hands forward and back in turn, with palms down (one hand moves forward while the other hand moves back, keep alternating).

26. Bring hands up by your shoulders with palms forward. Say "Heee!" stretching the vowel sound.

27. Move both hands together at waist height, palms down, horizontally in a slight arc, first to the left then to the right, following the arrows.

28. Palms remain down as you move both hands on the high left diagonal, then the same to the right side.

29. Repeat as above in 24. Then repeat text and gestures as in 25 through 29 (up through Hoo!) again.

30. Hands move together, making a small push to the front on the first hoosh, and then a larger push to the front on the second hoosh.

31. [silent movement]

32. [silent movement]

33. Pssssssst!

34. The little ghosts o' night are gone.

35. All have hidden, every one!

31. In silence, stretch arms to the sides and bring them up toward head; shield eyes with hands at brow and look searchingly, straight, then left, then right and straight ahead again.

32. Silently bring both hands behind ears, lowering eyelids, and listen a little while.

33. Bring right forefinger lightly to lips. After "psssssst" pause a little.

34. Bring hands up, palms facing front, not quite covering face. At "ghosts" start wiggling fingers while bringing hands down to the sides. At "gone" show open hands, as in "all gone."

35. At "All have hidden" hands disappear behind back. At "every one!" nod head.

Come to resting position.

Here you can hum or play the Quiet Fifth on the flute. You can either lie on the ground or move from child to child, rubbing each one's back tenderly.

Quiet Fifth

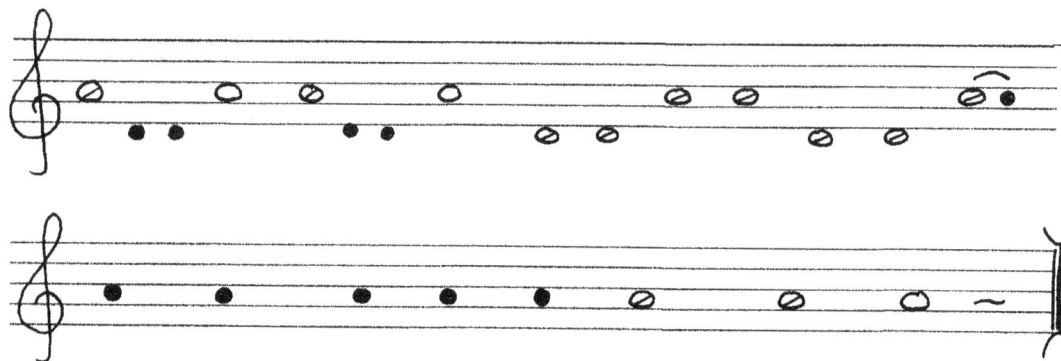

THE LITTLE GHOSTS O' NIGHT II
Spatial Movement Game

Text

Gestures
The game can begin in standing or sitting.

1. Dong-dong-dong-dong-dong-dong-dong-dong-dong-dong-dong-dong!

1. Suggest the striking of a bell by making a "clapper" with extended arms, the left hand cupped over the right fist, swinging back and forth; imagine the "clapper" striking the bell on each side.

2. M i d n i g h t !

2. After the twelfth stroke, slowly bring hands to each side of mouth, forming a megaphone, and call, "Midnight!"

3. Through the window panes

3. Arms and hands form a window through which the moon laughs.

4. the full moon laughs down bright.

4. Looking out the window, rest hands on sides of the head, framing it, and laugh. Continue laughing silently a while.

5. She woke them all right up,

5. Rub eyes with fingers.

6. the little ghosts o' night,
the little ghosts o' night.

6. Hold hands at eye level at sides of head, palms facing children, wiggling fingers in a lively way. Stoop a bit and pull back your head.

7. They swia - swia - sway

to the ghosties' roundalay:

swia - swia - sway,

swia - swia - sway.

7. With parallel hands moving together, palms down, at waist height, make a gently waving gesture up and down towards the right and towards the left, alternating lines, twice. Speak very melodically, almost singing.

8. Each wobbles his little head about,
the ghost o' night, the little lout.
Wi-wa-wobble, ni-na-nobble,
wi-wa-wobble, ni-na-nobble.

8. Stop where you have arrived. The head wobbles: from right to left and left to right, right to left and left to right. Continue wobbling for the next three lines, speaking rhythmically.

9. And swia - swia - sway
to the ghosties' roundalay:
swia - swia - sway,
swia - swia -sway.

10. They turn a-noola-noola-nile
around, around a little while:
Noola-noola-noola-nile,
noola-noola-noola-nile.

11. And swia - swia - sway
to the ghosties' roundalay:
swia - swia - sway,
swia - swia - sway.

12. The fingers of the ghosts,
     X   X

13. they tap on walls and posts.

14. Tasple - tasple, scrapple - scrapple,

tasple - tasple, scrapple - scrapple,

15. they scrapple: tasple - tasple - touse,

16. mysteriously all through the house

9. As above in 7.

10. Stop wherever you have arrived. With arms slightly flared at the sides and hands hanging loosely, indicate a "little dress." In this position, turn around your own axis over the course of two lines. (Two turns in total.) Let your arms wave slightly so that the "dress" flows.

11. As above in 7.

12. Hold hands up vertically, palms toward each other. In rhythm, lightly tap finger pads together at X.

13. For "wall": turn hands palms forward as if pressing against a wall, twice. For "posts," flex hands back so palms are up and move up as if pressing against an overhead post, twice.

14. Tap with all finger pads against posts above on each "Tasple, tasple." Scratch on the "walls" with all five fingers of each hand on each "scrapple," accent on s: *sssssscrapple*.

15. Continue as above, scratching with bent fingers on "scrapple" and tapping with outstretched fingers on "tasple" and "touse."

16. Hold hands parallel, palms down. Move hands down very slowly until they touch the floor, speaking mysteriously in whispers on "mysteriously all." Keeping hands parallel, move upward like two little parachutes floating up, draw out the vowel sounds as you whisper "through." On "house" indicate a roof with your two hands overhead.

Caution: It is important to note that the "mysterious" situation must be formed objectively through the sound and articulation of the voice. Movement should arise out of the music of sound and word and out of the speech rhythm. Avoid subjective emotion, mimicry and drama.

14. And swia - swia - sway ...

14. As in 7.

15. The good moon calls:
So long, so long, you ghosts o' night,
I must be gone!
They wave to her: So long, dear moon!
So -- so -- so long!

15. Wave lightly and loosely, continuously with the right hand.

16. Donnnnng!

16. With right hand over left fist strike forward: clapper against bell, allow the "nnnng" to sound for a long time while slowly raising fist.

17. From the clock tower,

17. Extend arms, hands held above the head, to form a clock tower.

18. it struck: One!

18. On "One!" show right fist with thumb out.

19. Hoo!

19. Pull back head slightly and lay rolled-up fists on right and left cheeks. Let out a soft, breathy "Hooo!"

20. Flisha-flisha-floosha-floosha,

20. Walk forward with raised hands (palms turned to the viewer) with hasty steps as if to call for help. Call out "Flisha-flisha-floosha-floosha" softly and cautiously.

21. flisha-flisha-floosha-floosha.

21. Crouch and put fists on cheeks, right and left. In this posture, take a few steps slowly and carefully, as if you don't want to be seen.

22. Hee!

22. From slightly curled fists, extends index fingers vertically upwards and hold them at eye level to the sides of head. Stretch the upper body and let out a cautious, stretched "Heee!"

23. To and fro:

23. With the fingertips of both hands, point to the left and say "to," then to the right and say "fro."

24. Hoosha-hoosha, hoosha-hoosha,
    (left)   (right)
hoosha-hoosha, hoosha-hoosha.

24. With mouse-like tripping steps, first scurry to the left, take enough time to change direction and

(left) (right)	
25. Hoo!	25. As in 19, then repeat 20 to 24.
26. Hoosh --- hoosh.	26. Stop suddenly and pull fists to chest. With the second "hoosh" crouch with a small jump and balance with hands on the floor.
27. Gone!	27. Kneel on the floor.
28. Hidden, every one!	28. Remain kneeling and either put your head in your hands just in front of your knees or cross your forearms on the floor just in front of your knees and rest your head on them. The ghosts are gone.

then scurry to the right. Repeat.

Here the Quiet Fifth can be hummed or played on the flute. The educator either lies on the floor or goes from child to child and gently strokes each one's back.

Quiet Fifth

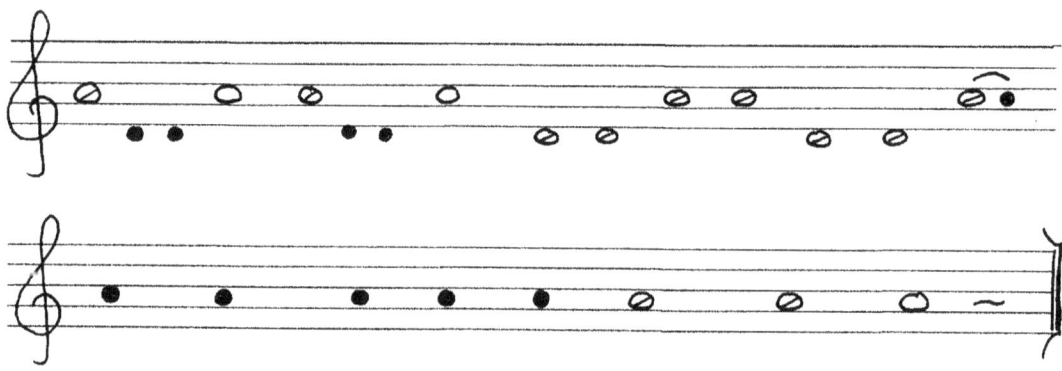

RECOMMENDATIONS FOR COMPANION/BRIDGE VERSES
Little rhythmical-musical stories without gestures

With these or similar verses you can bridge easily from one game to another without losing the rhythmic-musical thread of the speech.

A. Bridge to Gnome Tinkletong

Ting-ting-ting-ting-ting-ting-ting!
What sounds so clear and bright?
Ting-ting-ting-ting-ting-ting-ting!
I think it's Tinkletong the Gnome,
Who hammers in his Mountain Home

— Mood of the fifth song, "In the Mountain" (see p. 33)

B. Bridge to "In Woodland a Soft Crack"

Listen, I still hear it.
Kneck dee kneck, what could it be?
Kneck and knack, do you hear that?
I think it's the Gnome in the fir tree.

— "In Woodland a Soft Crack" hand gesture game (p. 40)

C. Bridge (Companion) to Giant Rummelgood

Listen, I still hear it (or: hear it again).
Rom and rum and rom and rum!
Is it maybe Rummelgood?

— "Who Tromps Around Through All the Wood?" (p. 68)

D. Bridge or companion verse for use with instruments

We invite our flute (harp) to play!
During rest (play, dance, hop, etc.) the flute (harp) will stay.

or:

Let's listen once, how the flute plays the hopping game.
(The teacher plays once while the children listen.)
With the flute, we can play the hopping game.
(Begin the game.)

E. Bridge from rest to the repeat of the game or starting a new game

Rested, rested
We all have rested.
Soon starts the little man
To hammer again in the land.

or:
To be a gnome was grand,
Let's be a giant in the land.

Wilma Ellersiek
A Life for Rhythm

In a small village in Schleswig-Holstein, directly on the coastline of the Baltic Sea, on June 15, 1921, Wilma Ellersiek first saw the light of the world. With the rhythm of the waves, the murmur of the wind, and with dogs, cats, chickens, ducks, and a horse as playmates, she lived a childhood bound up with nature. Her friends were, as she said, flowers, trees, sand and stars. But above all, rhythm, encountered at the seaside in many-layered forms, would stay with Wilma Ellersiek throughout her life. Looking back, she perceived her childhood as an almost heavenly life in the rhythm of nature. In her parents' home she was encouraged to pursue music, but also language and literature. Nature on one hand and culture on the other were an ideal, marvelous and edifying atmosphere for developing one's humanity.

In 1927 the Ellersiek family moved to Westphalia. Again little Wilma had the luck of living next door to a farm, so the dear creatures remained her friends as before. New, however, was the impression of grain fields waving in the breeze, another rhythmic wave movement. Now came early meetings with other children, first in kindergarten and soon also in school. Their time together was filled with singing, dancing, and recitation; indeed, looking back she sees her entire childhood and youth as suffused with music and rhythm a sound basis for her later activity.

Wilma Ellersiek completed her schooldays with the Abitur examination and in 1941 she began to study in Leipzig, beginning in the major areas of school music, German philology, and history of art. Serious sickness forced her to interrupt her study. This was followed by the confusion of wartime, near the end of which, in 1945, her family was forced to flee from Eastern Europe. In Essen, Wilma Ellersiek resumed her study at the Volkwang School, albeit changing her major field. Her new field of study was rhythmic-musical education, continued in Stuttgart at the State Academy

for Music and Performing Arts. There she became a student of Elfriede Feudel, herself a master student of the founder of "Eurhythmics," Émile Jaques-Dalcroze.* In addition to studying eurhythmics, Wilma Ellersiek also entered the study of speech education and completed both fields in 1957 with the state examination. Eurhythmics then became her life's work. She remained at the Stuttgart Music Academy as an assistant in the three departments: Eurhythmics, Theater, and Spoken Word. After her time as assistant, she was offered a lecturing position, and later a professorship. In addition to her work at the Academy, she worked as stage director in opera and drama in Stuttgart, Vienna and London, among other places.

Again a serious sickness caused a decisive change in vocation, and again it was rhythm that fascinated her. Wilma Ellersiek now turned to research on the specific effects of rhythm and movement, language and music on the small child.

---

* Dalcroze's Eurhythmics are not to be confused with the art of movement developed by Rudolf Steiner, called "Eurythmy."

Her work on this theme provoked attention, and in 1968 she received a research commission for it from the State of Baden-Württemberg. Out of this impulse the first "gesture games" for the preschool child were born. Out of these little gesture games, step by step, with enviable intuition, and also with enormous exactitude and care, she developed great, connected play-units in rhyme, interwoven with rhythm and music. In the beginning she called her courses "School for Parents," for her idea was to teach children together with mothers or fathers. In the late 1960s, the Stuttgart Music Academy established for Wilma Ellersiek, within the Eurhythmics Department, the specialty "Eurhythmics for the Preschool Age." During this time, a meeting took place with the "matriarch" of the Waldorf kindergartens, Klara Hattermann, with whom she maintained an intimate friendship. Klara Hattermann viewed the new games with interest, accompanied Wilma Ellersiek through many difficulties and encouraged again and again her continued activity. Along with several of Wilma Ellersiek's students from Stuttgart, Klara Hattermann carried the games into the world through workshops. After 25 years of intensive teaching activity, Wilma Ellersiek retired, leaving the Academy in 1983. Lifted out of her teaching responsibilities, she became more creative than ever. Many of the games were developed at this time, among which are all the caresses and many lullabies. Additionally, during this time, a circle of interested friends came together in Hannover around Klara Hattermann to work intensively with the games of Wilma Ellersiek and see to their propagation in a form as true as possible to the intention of their author.

The games of Wilma Ellersiek came from her listening to nature; in a way true to their origin she succeeded in artistically molding speech, rhythm and the corresponding gestures to bring the wind, flowers, beasts, sun, moon, and stars into the child's presence through little musical tales. In this way through the swinging, healing, natural rhythms of the games, she offered something to today's children from her own nature-filled childhood.

— Ingrid Weidenfeld

CONTRIBUTORS

Ingrid Weidenfeld, German edition editor
Ingrid Weidenfeld was born in Stuttgart, where she studied Dalcroze eurhythmics and violin at the State Academy for Music and Performing Arts. Within the regular eurhythmics course she completed special studies with Wilma Ellersiek on the subject of eurhythmics for preschool children. She went on to work with parent-and-child groups at a family education center, as well as giving violin lessons at a music school for young people. Later she taught at the college for music and performance arts in Stuttgart, specializing in the Ellersiek model for preschool eurhythmics, while continuing to give courses for preschool children and parents. Ingrid is the founder of INSEL (Institute for Wilma Ellersiek's Gesture Games), dedicated to bringing Wilma Ellersiek's gesture games and plays to as many people as possible. In 2001 she founded a training course in Stuttgart for the hand gesture games by Wilma Ellersiek. See www.handgestenspiele.de.

Birgit Krohmer, Contributor
Birgit Krohmer is a Waldorf kindergarten teacher, eurythmist, and therapeutic eurythmist in Germany, a visiting lecturer at higher education institutions in Germany and internationally, and an IASWECE Council member.

Somer Serpe, Translator and Editor
After growing up in Europe and Japan, Somer trained as an artist and as a teacher, earning her BFA degree at Parsons School of Design and her Masters in Waldorf Early Childhood Education at Sunbridge College. She taught Nursery and Kindergarten at the Great Barrington Rudolf Steiner School for 15 years, and now leads an outdoor Parent and Child program. Somer is the Early Childhood Assistant Program director and a faculty member at Sound Circle Center for Arts and Anthroposophy, and a Northeast Regional Representative for WECAN. Somer and her husband raised their two daughters in the Berkshires where they both attended Waldorf schools. She loves bringing Ellersiek games to the children and parents in her program and enjoys gardening, puppetry, singing and creating healing stories for children and parents.

Lynn St. Pierre, Translator and Editor
Lynn St. Pierre joyfully presents developmental movement in the form of loving touch, hand gesture and large movement plays and Spacial Dynamics at Waldorf teacher training centers, conferences and schools internationally. Lynn is a certified trainer in the developmental movement for early childhood created by Wilma Ellersiek and a Spacial Dynamics Teacher Trainer. She was the founding teacher of the Apple Song Kindergarten Parent Collective in Lyons, Colorado and has taught Nursery and Toddler classes in the Pacific Northwest.

Kundry Willwerth, Translator
Kundry Willwerth (1932-2017) was a Waldorf kindergarten teacher for over 30 years. She directed Magic Garden Puppets, a marionette theater group which performed throughout central New York State. She presented workshops throughout North America and internationally. Kundry was a founding member of the Stuttgart Hand Gesture Working Circle and trained teacher-trainers from the United States, Canada, Brazil, Europe, and Australia. She translated and edited four previous books of gesture games by Wilma Ellersiek, also available from WECAN (*Giving Love, Bringing Joy*; *Gesture Games for Spring and Summer*; *Gesture Games for Autumn and Winter*; and *Dancing Hand, Trotting Pony*). After her death, her work on this final volume was taken up and completed by colleagues.

Addresses

Vereinigung der Waldorfkindergärten e.V.
(German Association of Waldorf Kindergartens)
www.waldorfkindergarten.de
info@waldorfkindergarten.de

**Institut für die Spiele
von Wilma Ellersiek e.V.**
(German institute for the games by Wilma Ellersiek)
www.handgestenspiele.de
info@handgestenspiele.de
insel-verein@t-online.de

**Waldorf Early Childhood Association
of North America (WECAN)**
www.waldorfearlychildhood.org
info@waldorfearlychildhood.org

**International Association for Steiner/Waldorf
Early Childhood Education (IASWECE)**
www.iaswece.org
info@iaswece.org

www.ingramcontent.com/pod-product-compliance
Lightning Source LLC
Chambersburg PA
CBHW081459070526
44586CB00019B/2421